No. 36

# Nectar of Nondual Truth

## CONTENTS

**10 Learning to Live Under Water**
*by Rabbi Rami Shapiro*
The presence of Divine Reality permeates all worlds, and exists eternally beyond the worlds as well. On earth, that presence is just more difficult of recognition, requiring forbearance blended with willingness to see.

**12 The Triple Gem of Vedanta**
*by Babaji Bob Kindler*
The ancient and timeless path of India, often referred to as the Sanatana Dharma, or "Eternal Religion," sports several main facets which reveal many divine faces. Three of these are notable and, when examined closely, are well nigh impossible to separate out.

**15 The Three Blind Men & the Elephant**
*by Rev. Chris VonLobedan*
The world of religion is elephant-like, having various parts — like a tail, a trunk, a stout leg, etc. — and living beings are like blind men groping about, finding one part, then basing their often narrow conclusions accordingly....as this article so aptly explains.

**18 The Virtue of Truthfulness**
*by Swami Brahmeshananda*
Whereas appearances are in the very nature of the world of name and form, Truth, Sat, or Satyam, is the hidden foundation behind them all. Lovers and knowers of Divine Realty strive to bring what is hidden forward so that all beings may be established in It and leave off suffering with what is essentially unreal.

**25 The Role of Peace in Healing**
*by Bhavatarini Ma Jocelyne Neilsen*
Sri Sarada told us; "Nothing worthwhile can be had without peace of mind." In this article, a lifelong practitioner of both the healing arts and spiritual life reveals the inner dynamics of this hearty combination.

**27 An Interview with Mother Teresa**
*by Lex Hixon*
In an interview with Mother Teresa for his "In The Spirit" program on WBAI Radio, Lex Hixon was able to ask this holy personage important and revealing questions about her life and times.

**37 Do Not Worry: Nature is Fine**
*by Roshi Hogen Bays*
The inherent perfection that is Existence is termed "silent, non-two" (moku-funi) in Zen. Thus it is nondual (shoso-funi). Its experience abides in one, eternal moment (ichinen-mannen). Simply put, then, everything is fine.....

**38 The Relationship Between Judaism & The Spiritual Technologies of India**
*by Jeffrey Rothman*
Meditation is the Life of Formless Reality. It is and has been used, consciously and unconsciously, since Being took egos and bodies and inhabited the realms of name and form. Here, all religions on earth can benefit from Mother India's long-standing teachings and mastery of this most unique and subtle of spiritual artforms.

**41 The Special Esoteric Significance of Sarasvati & Her Veena**
*by Swami Sunirmalananda*
When the Divine Mother of the Universe expresses Her infinite nature through the music of Her sacred Veena, worlds effloresce and beings sport in bliss.

**45 Sri Krishna's Instructions on Nonorigination**
*by Brother Tadrupa*
Containing so many fine teachings on multiple levels, and with so many perspectives gracing Sri Krishna's sacred song, the Bhagavad Gita, we must be sure to partake deeply of the nondual strands of Advaita running in and throughout its enlightening slokas.

**47 The Qualified Mind**
*by Annapurna Sarada*
The seriousness of a strong spiritual life and practice, and the need for a competent guide, is only surpassed by the necessity of a qualified mind. For, without that, the former two boons might very likely come to naught.

*"....it is not enough to stand by and simply wonder about how to lead humanity into the higher echelons of Nonduality. That path has already been well laid out by Mother India, has been available over endless phases of time (kalpas) and nurtured as such by Its many luminaries who have realized It."*

# Publisher's Page

Sarada Ramakrishna Vivekananda – SRV Associations
*"Setting the feet of humanity on the path of Universal Truth."*

### Notes on an Advaitic Journal

At the basis of Advaita as the philosophy of Shankara and his gurus, there is Advaita as experience. Advaita as experience represents that supreme place where all diversity merges in its Essence. It is not combatant or immiscible with qualified or dualistic approaches, but rather provides them their place of consummate arrival. Where actual practice rather than mere book learning is emphasized, where religion, philosophy and spirituality are not separate from one another, where knowledge and love, reason and devotion, are never divorced from each other, there does the truth of authentic nonduality effloresce.

Historically speaking, experiential Advaita originated with the ancient Rishis. Therefore, the Upanisads contain the nondual truths of the Vedas which declare: idam mahabhutam anantam aparam vijnanaghana eva, *"This great Being is endless and without limit. It is a mass of indivisible Consciousness only."*

### SRV Associations & Universality

The SRV Associations are part of a worldwide movement of spiritual aspirants devoted to the study and practice of Vedanta and Divine Mother Wisdom. The ideals of this ancient pathway to God, exemplified in the lives of Sri Sarada Devi, Sri Ramakrishna and Swami Vivekananda, are the original and eternal perfection of the Soul and its inherent oneness with Reality, the manifesting of divinity in our lives, selfless service of all beings as God, and reverence for the ultimate unity of all sacred traditions. To this end our purpose is to study, worship, and contemplate Truth so that spirituality may flourish. This is the Advaitic way — *"None else but Self, none other than Mother."*

### Nectar's Mission — *Advaita-Satya-Amritam*

In Sanskrit, *amrita*, nectar also means Immortality – and this is, indeed, what we are offering: opportunities to become aware of this Amrita that is our very Essence via the rarefied teachings from Vedanta and the World Religions and Philosophies that appear in each issue of Nectar.

Nectar of Non-Dual Truth is SRV Associations' heartfelt offering of highest Wisdom to the human community. It is the sincerest form of love and service we know to disseminate nondual Truth and teachings which transmit pure knowledge, pure love, and true universality. Through Nectar we are working out SRV's mission of spiritual upliftment and education. Please join us; this is a universal movement.

### Keeping Nectar in Print

Nectar is a free magazine that can be ordered in printed form online at www.srv.org, and it can also be viewed online. (play.google.com/books) However, substantial donations are needed every year to maintain this publication in print. Why is this important?

1 – Printed Nectars are best for person to person and organization to organization dissemination of these ennobling teachings that deepen one's own spiritual life and engender knowledge of, acceptance, and reverence for all other paths.

2 – Only printed copies can reach those who do not have access to online viewing, including prison inmates, who are a particular focus of SRV's social seva.

Use the subscription/donation form provided at the back of this issue to send a check or credit card payment to SRV Associations, P.O. Box 1364, Honokaa, HI., 96727, or donate online at www.srv.org. Your donations are tax deductible.

---

With reverent gratitude, we heartily thank the contributing writers of this issue of Nectar of Nondual Truth, who have so graciously and selflessly shared the wisdom of their respective traditions and practices.

---

## Staff of Nectar of Nondual Truth

**Publisher**
Sarada Ramakrishna Vivekananda Associations
an Annual Publication
For more information concerning the SRV Associations or Nectar of Nondual Truth please contact:
SRV Associations, PO Box 1364, Honoka'a, HI 96727
Phone: (808) 990-3354
e-mail: srvinfo@srv.org   website: www.srv.org
Nectar Subscription is on a donation basis only

No part of this publication may be reproduced or transmitted in any form without permission from the publisher. Entire contents copyright 2021. All Rights Reserved. ISSN 1531-1414

**Editor**
Babaji Bob Kindler

**Associate Editor**
Annapurna Sarada

**Production**
Lokelani Kindler

**Cover Image:**
Alia Gurtov

**Acknowledgement**
*Image of Ramakrishna's Disciples
Courtesy of Vedanta Press
800-816-2242*

**Contributing Writers**
Swami Brahmeshananda
Swami Sunirmalananda
Roshi Hogen Bays
Rev. Chris VonLobedan
BhavatariniMa Jocelyne Nielsen
Rabbi Rami Shapiro
Annapurna Sarada
Brother Tadrupa
Jeffrey Rothman
Alexander Hixon
Babaji Bob Kindler

# EDITORIAL

Dharma holds a strong and crucial place in the realm of knowledge. There is secular knowledge, what the Indians rishis called aparavidya. Then there is jnanam proper, which is wisdom gleaned by the illumined minds of the world's religions, and that is found in the scriptures of the same. In India there is also Atmajnan, which is highest wisdom associated only with direct spiritual experience of Brahman, the Formless Reality. Of course, and requiring careful consideration, there is mithyajnana, or false knowledge. It is, at least, a good tool to utilize when one is searching for authentic wisdom. As Sri Krishna states in the Bhagavad Gita, the seers come to know both the truth and the non-truth, so that "The Real" can get accented and singled out in and of Itself, with no competitors around It.

In and amidst all these forms of knowledge, the dharma stands forth as being readily accessible to a larger percentage of humanity, providing a stepping stone leading beyond morality and ethics, as well. That is why Nectar of Nondual Truth has spent several decades exposing teachings to struggling souls, seeking souls, and souls who are already well along the path of qualified Wisdom leading to Nonduality. For, it is certainly not possible to place pure Advaita in words, to describe the Indescribable. Nonetheless, the fine spiritual art of "Sphota" is called "shabda-advaita," meaning that what is inherent in words sheds the light of understanding on all that they signify. The word "sphut" in Sanskrit translates as "that which bursts forth," which in the case of dharmic words of inner power means they illumines what they infer — both in terms of light and sound.

Therefore, the potent utterances coming forth from the lips of the luminaries over phases of time, found recorded in the scriptures of the various religious traditions of the world, have great weight for counterbalancing the always accumulating store of ignorance gathering in the human mind — if not doing away with it completely and for all time. For example, the writers who gathered together their own stores of wisdom in order to complete this issue of Nectar are herein expressing everything from the presence of nature, to specific spiritual practices, to the role and presence of the gods and goddesses, and right on up and in to the prime subject of nonduality itself. It would seem, then, or is apparent, that all the world's religions hold wisdom of many different levels of deeper understanding which, when contemplated over time, show the connections leading to nonduality.

Therefore, it is not enough to stand by and simply wonder about how to lead humanity into the higher echelons of Nonduality. That path has already been well laid out by Mother India, has been available over endless phases of time (kalpas) and nurtured as such by her many luminaries who have realized It. As Swami Vivekananda, the New Prophet of Nonduality, has told us recently in our history: "All old, foggy forms of religion are mere outworn superstitions. Why struggle to keep them alive? Why give people dirty ditch-water to drink whilst the River of Life and Truth flows by?"

So take in copious amounts of dharmic wisdom and contemplate and integrate it well into life. Surface thoughts and the habit of superficial thinking will then dissolve, and remembrance of better times, finer atmospheres, and higher truths will dawn, accordingly. This path of enlightened words and illumined thoughts will carry the soul right up to the thrilling threshold of nondual access. One more step inwards and the apparently individualized soul merges with the Supreme Soul — its very Self. Then the forceful words will echo forth within you, "Welcome back. You were never apart from Me in the first place; you merely dreamed of a separation...."

*Om Peace, Peace, Peace*

*Babaji Bob Kindler*

Babaji in South India

# NECTAR OF ADVAITIC INSTRUCTION

## Questions from Our Readers

*In today's spiritual circles, questions from students consist basically of mayic components. Matters concerning daily life, obstacles to success and suffering coming seemingly from nowhere, take precedence. Among sincere practitioners, however, the subject is all about Nonduality, and the methods and practices necessary to attain It.*

**"Can you go into more depth about this process — What is the difference between dissolution and destruction; and When Kali merges with Shiva, is that when all returns to pure Self, until a new cycle begins? And also, how much of this is allegorical and how much is literal?"**

Dissolution is the truth; destruction is the appearance. Conditionally, "destruction" happens only to those who do not know their birthless, deathless, Atman.

When Mother retreats into Brahman/Paramasiva at the end of a yuga, or Mahayuga, all "things" go back to seeds/bijams in unmanifested prakriti, and all "beings" return to Brahman. However, those "beings" who have ignorantly remained focused on matter only, for so many lifetimes, though they are always in Brahman, do not consciously merge into Brahman, but return to material realms for more "birth and death." This is the literal reading of life in cycles. Waking up from the cosmic dream is rare. That is why Sri Krishna states in the Gita, *"Of a thousand beings who hear of Me, only one of these seeks Me, and of a thousand of those seekers, only one comes to Me."*

Sri Ramakrishna has given us the story of an old woman who takes a walk on the beach in front of Her house every morning. She keeps her eye on the sands and picks up little items such as pieces of glass, sea foam, etc., and takes them home with her. She then puts them all in a huge glass jar, filled with such items. These represent the souls that Mother has selected for the next cycle of time. They are caught in maya due to their own preoccupation with the sands of time and space.....

**"What does it mean to come from the ancestors via lower heaven?"**
The ancestors who did not strive for and gain enlightenment in their previous lifetime attend upon lower heaven after death. They return to earth to work out their negative karma after the merit of their good karmas get exhausted. Some get free and attend higher worlds, never to return to earth again.

**"Where can I think of the curtain of nescience existing within the mind/body mechanism?**
It is thickest in the lower mind that is worldly and that does not take refuge in God while the soul is in the body. It is subtler and thinner as realization of higher truth gets accomplished, giving an opportunity for attaining highest Reality, i.e., Moksha.

**"Where do these prior lifetime memories go if they were stripped from my awareness via the curtain of nescience?**
Into the subconscious or unconscious mind. If intense practices are utilized while the soul is embodied, they an be recovered, or remembered.

**"If the curtain of nescience was thick enough for me to be birthed in relative ignorance, does this mean that I was born with a samskara for fear, brooding, and ignorance, which is also evidenced by my choice of womb and culture?"**
Yes. Most all beings here on earth have samskaras, positive, negative, and mixed. Accenting the former and neutralizing the two latter helps the soul to destroy old conditionings and karmas lodged in the mind. Doing sadhana in this lifetime will attenuate or remove old samskaras — which is the work at hand to be done.

**"When it comes to nirvitarka samapatti – when the vrittis in the mind leading to meaning and coming in from the sense organs have ceased and one is identifying with the knower – I have found that when one ceases the vrittis in the mind in the forms of thoughts and subtle visualizations there are still subtle vrittis that exist. After contemplation it seems that the ahamkara and buddhi maintain their vibration even in the absence of thoughts and visualizations in the mind. It also seems like there are subtle vrittis in the manas aspect of the antahkarana in the absence of thoughts and thought forms as well. How does one quell these residual vrittis of the various mechanisms of the four-fold mind? I immediately think that through purification and utilizing the Seven Ways of Mastering Consciousness these residual vibrations will be lessened leading to deeper meditation. I would greatly appreciate your thoughts and advice on this — I will implement direction immediately."**
The one word is constancy — one of Holy Mother's favorites. All is accomplished with its presence or, put obversely, nothing can really fructify without it. That is the conclusion of the Father of Yoga as well. He puts it in terms of the presence of very subtle samskaras, i.e., vrittis, even after the seventh limb of steady meditation has been gained. This is also true of the gunas, that is, they also remain and re-insinuate themselves despite the aspirant's best efforts. The way I explain that, is that if the soul wrought all manner of karmas for lifetimes, then an equal

amount of effort in the opposite direction will need to be put forth to reverse the effects. But do not fret; you have the Great Master at your back, as also the Vedanta. One lifetime can be enough time to neutralize all — but not without constancy (once you have found the Guru, the sangha, and the dharma teachings).

"I've been contemplating the existence of Maya in terms of how this universe of Time, Space, Causation, Name and Form come to be. I've understood this as just like a mirage in the desert; only due to the presence and existence of the desert does the mirage exist. But one cannot say that the mirage has any true existence. Again, I've heard of Maya existing due to the 'closeness' to Brahman and through its very proximity that it shines/exists through borrowed light. There still remains the thought that, why does this phenomenon even occur, for what purpose if it is unreal? When I think about these questions I come to the conclusion (please correct any deluded understanding) that the very notion of 'does Maya exist or not' comes from the standpoint of ignorance and thus one's comprehension of the fact of maya is thereby deluded because it (maya) is being questioned from the standpoint of taking it as real (because the questioner is still attached to the body or mind thereby still entrapped by maya). As Shankara said maya is inscrutable. Nevertheless, when one transcends Maya, the mirage is seen for what it truly is - unreal. Thence forth, maya no longer exists and Lila is engaged in — is my thinking about this correct? Please enlighten my thought process."

Yes, your thinking is coming along very well along the lines of this slippery slope of a subject. As you approach the nondual conclusions, after your intense study period and self-inquiry is done and gels, you will feel the deeper element of finer comprehension around maya dawn in your mind. I have put it lately that higher awareness does not see maya anymore for all has become Brahman to It. It is lower and conditioned consciousness that courts maya and its risks, and its subtleties. There was a very good exchange on this topic at the class today, which is why you should learn how to work the new website and take in the new and ongoing events. Are your time restraints restricting you from doing that?

"Mother's Essence is the Kundalini energy which flows through the points of concentrated spiritual force along the spine. I was born with many spinal problems that I continue to work on fixing — can that affect the nature/manner/frequency of kundalini energy?"

Yes, but it does not have to. Kundalini— unbeknownst to many seekers — is not a physical energy whatsoever. She does not have to use the physical spine to accomplish Her mission, to be sure. So think more of Heart and Head/Mind when you think of Her rising in you.

"I have been contemplating the teaching of neti neti a lot over the past few weeks. I can see and feel the importance of discrimination, of constantly checking within to be sure that I am only identifying with That which never changes, Brahman. The birthless, deathless, eternally blissful reality that is our true Self. I understand that the practice of neti neti leads to a genuine realization that all this is Brahman. Is it good to acknowledge that all this is Brahman even while I am practicing discrimination and before I have completely overcome all my identification with the body/mind mechanism?"

When the luminaries make a statement such as, "All is Brahman," the import is that Brahman underlies everything; It is not a "thing" in Itself. It is not matter, energy, or thought, yet It is the foundation for all three. Since most practitioners are not clear about this yet, and either mix up God with mammon or are in the stages of recovering from th dark influences of maya/false superimposition, the neti neti practice keeps them honest and clear about the facts. Further, there is every reason to hold neti neti and All is Brahman together in one complete view, particularly since this world is the densest and most difficult to transcend. Go forward in this way, and inquire from good sources as well to keep the picture always clear.

"I was reading a little in the Vivekachudamani tonight. In some of the early verses Shankara uses the term bodha-chaksu. Is this a synonym of jnana-chaksu as used in the Gita? Are there any little differences in emphasis when the former is used?"

I see no reason why the two terms should not be held synonymous. If any distinction be made, it might be one of the all-seeing eye being allocated more to vision in the Gita's case, but more to Intelligence in Shankara's.

"In studying the Gita, it has come clear that the Lord advises refuge in Ishvara in the practice of the various yogas leading to realization of Brahman. Whether it is karma, jnana, bhakti, or raja yoga, He instructs us to use Ishvara in various ways, and even synthesizes these paths through Ishvara. Is this a mature understanding?"

Yes. *"One gets to the Father through the Son"* is a good way of saying it. As described before, only masterful meditators, what Lord Vasishtha calls the "Walker of the Skies," can move straight into Brahman, with no intermediary — which does not mean that the intermediary (Ishvara/Ishvari) disappears, or is not needed anymore. There are steps to Heaven, and some of them are major, all-abiding ones. Sri Ramakrishna likens Ishvara forms to icebergs that do not melt under the sun due to their vast bulk and hard consistency. As these special icebergs survive the rising and falling of the sun daily, so too does Ishvara/Ishvari survive the passing of yugas, and even the Mahayuga. Thus, humanity always remembers It/Them when cycles pick up again after Mahapralaya.

"May I please get the chant (with translation) used to begin a class that is about 'going for refuge in that Brahman which turns the light of understanding toward the Atman?' I need to start learning more chants now the 28 are memorized, at least to the basic level."

Yes, here it is. And we should go through it in person so that you get the recitation and intonation of it correctly:
AUM

*yo brahmanam vidadhati purvam*
*yo vai vedamscha prahinoti tasmai*
*tam ha deva atma buddhi prakasham*
*mumuksurvai sharanamaham prapadye*

"That One, formless Being, out which sprang the Trinity at the beginning of a cosmic cycle, and who granted the Vedas unto Lord Brahma. Who is the eternal bridge to Immortality. Who is partless, formless, actionless, and divine. Who resembles fire that has consumed all its fuel. Seeking liberation, I go for refuge into that Supreme Brahman, whose Light turns the understanding of mankind towards the Atman, the indivisible Self in all."

**"In meditating, chanting, sadhana, etc., is it good to have ego-death as a goal? As in, 'If I continue to walk this path and pursue higher wisdom and do sadhana/worship/japa ego-death will inevitably occur in some degree, either via my own efforts or by an act of God's grace?' Odd how I found the notion of death to be a fearful thing, and yet ego-death is something that, even though it feels like a cessation of me, it also sounds like it would bring incredible liberation from worldly burdens. I yearn for it, and also feel a degree of unfamiliarity and uncertainty regarding it, and wonder how I can bridge that gap of fearing the unknown unless I just outright experience it by pushing harder. I know I'm not supposed to fear the illusion of death, whether speaking of physical or ego, but the natural tendency to flee seems very strong, like a knee-jerk, ingrained survival mechanism. I hope that makes sense. It's just that, with the inevitability of mortal death (or what we call death traditionally) I am left with two choices: The imperfect ego of me, or Self. And I feel a constant battle to go back and forth and it gets hairy sometimes. Me, I think I know pretty well."**

Probably best not to associate the ego's death with the body's death, and thus confuse the issue. The body has its own predestined time to disappear. That can scarcely be altered. What we want is the death of ignorance, for that will make all of life divine, and death will not occur to us. This is the secret of those who love Mother; they simply sport in Her eternally.

**"As one in the householder lifestyle, how much is an appropriate amount of time to dedicate to meditation, scripture reading, japa, and other yoga (a bit related to the last question. Since moving and getting a more demanding job, I feel as though I've lost a bit of that spiritual depth and am eager to bring it back. One example is fasting. Mormons fast every first Sunday of the month, and I've decided to bring that back because I always felt great blessings come from it. Do you fast? Do you follow conventional Hindu fasting and other calendar events like the Ekadasi? Could/should I get into this too?"**

To start, give one part of the mind to work, one part to study of scripture, one part to serving the guru, and one part to meditation. The hard part of this is reducing work, due to the "need" for money. But most people do not know that they can live on less, and that giving more time to spiritual practice will right the balance naturally so that money comes spontaneously. They do not trust God, and rely instead on the world. Trusting, then, becomes like a pregnant woman whose work is taken away from her by her in-laws in increments as she nears the time of birthing her child. In like manner, work, too, comes to a timely end.

Regarding fasting, it is an inferior austerity, not even mentioned in the Gita by the Lord. Instead, he commends worship and sacrifice as the best bodily austerities. Of course, the mindset in which one does works and tapas is important, so fasting can be accomplished for better reasons, by higher mind.

**"When Kali is standing on Shiva's corpse, is this encompassing the idea that Kali is unobserved Shakti, and that's why she is chaos? i.e., if Shiva ceases to observe the cosmos, destruction abounds?"**

First, let's say instead, "Siva's subtle body," not "corpse," since He knows not any death. As for the true meaning of the cosmic scene you cite here, no, it is that Siva has seen Her, and has slipped into samadhi due to beholding Her vision. If that vision is deep enough, and it is time for a yuga to end, then dissolution (not destruction) may occur. When it does, She Herself states (*Srimad Devi Bhagavatam*) that She merges into Him until the beginning of the next yuga.

**"When it comes to the stance of Indifference/Upekshanam towards those that are evil/unrighteous, is this more of a benevolent indifference whereby the aspirant is concentrating on the other's svarupa and thereby seeing past their faults? Would you say this reasoning is along the correct lines? If one was simply to be 'indifferent' I can see how some minds may default to a sort of curt indifference which is simply influencing tamasic vrittis, which would be missing the point of purifying the mind (rendering the vrittis sattvic and quelling them entirely)."**

For personal growth and safety of the aspirant in the practice stages, indifference amounts to staying clear of such beings as far as possible. Read the chapter in the Gita (#16) wherein The Lord speaks about the Divine and Demoniacal for more clarity around this. Further, it might look all well and good to say that the Atman is within evil beings too, but since It is not realized in them, and deeply buried, they are dangerous. Even "good" people are dangerous to one another (say, a "loving" spouse, etc.), so what to speak of the obviously evil souls. Looking about to see the horrors that mankind submits other beings to on this earth is enough to leave forgiveness out of the picture. There is no excuse for such actions. It sounds like you understand this well enough, and so escape that net of naivete that some fall into around this subject."

**"'A pin must at least prick where a sword was destined to fall.' Is this a statement of God's grace, or mercy? Is it similar to when Sri Ramakrishna says 'tears shed for God wash the sins of previous births.' Do small negative karmic actions result in small irritations happening to a person, or can they build up over time or is it really just unknown, and up to God to deliver accordingly? Also related, is it possible for a person to recognize instant karmic reactions, which suggest their karma buildup has waned and is happening in real time, indicating they're closer to equilibrium?"**

Holy Mother's statement that you cite is given regarding the efficacy of using the mantra in practice. It diminishes the effects of karma. And yes, those little karmas are called "mortar and pestle" karmas, and mount up from a number of small acts. They surface, for instance, in family life, causing all manner of squabbles and such. Further, the more advanced a spiritual aspirant becomes, the quicker his or her karmas return to them. That is why beings who are not mature reap karmas later, and get confused because they have forgotten the source of them.

**"The Bhagavad Gita says no spiritual effort goes unnoticed. I sometimes feel very close to the Truth when meditating and have a feeling of spirituality that lasts where I have a good deal of patience and insight, and then sometimes out of the blue find myself backsliding into anger and other embarrassingly petty egotistical behavior. What is the solution to this? Deeper sadhana, more consistency? Are some passions only capable of being eliminated by renunciation?"**

This is somewhat similar to everyday actions, i.e., that some actions we do are simple and commonplace, and others are intense. The intense ones have a more lasting effect. And yes, deeper sadhana is the solution. However, and importantly, practice must be well guided by a luminary, thus not influenced by, and kept independent of, the unripe ego. Aspirants should not try and intensify an impure mind, like unwisely going on a 30 day retreat when their guru told them to meditate intensely for one hour, twice a day — this is an example of the type of foolhardiness that "self-guided" aspirants engage in today. They think they know what is best for them, sort of like the little child who ignores his parents when they tell him not to play near the edge of the cliff in the woods outback."

**"Initiation, given at the auspicious moment to a receptive aspirant, signals the immediate or impending finale to the cycles of birth and death within the limited realms of relativity. What does initiation look like? Have you initiated many individuals? What expectations come with it?"**

It is accomplished, ideally early in life, on a holy day, preselected by the guru after the matter has been agreed upon by both parties. At that time the mantra is transmitted, and that signals an end to rebirth on earth — particularly if the mantra gets utilized by the student, and not discarded or forgotten. There are three Goddesses (Tripura Sundari) involved in this best of all processes. The first is the physical image; the second, the visualized image who appears later, after practice has been ongoing for some time. The third is formless Reality. Thus, the mantra, well utilized, leads to liberation.

**"In studying sutra 17 of Patanjali's Yoga, with the commentary, it seems clear that he has aligned the lower samadhis with the cosmic principles more or less from gross to subtle. Vitarka being the gross elements etc. Does it follow then that the master meditator experiences all levels of samadhis when performing the dissolving the mind stream meditation?"**

Such a versatile being can certainly shift easily among the levels of consciousness, which is another way of saying samadhi. For, even objects represent a state of consciousness, and therefore a type of samadhi. It only depends upon individual awareness to see them as such, instead of seen as being mundane, pain-bearing, burdened by pleasure, etc. A simultaneous experience of all samadhis, if one could describe it that way, would be ultimate Awareness, wherein every "thing" cancelled itself out. Otherwise, the meditator has to shift from mode to mode, mood to mood, samadhi to samadhi, accordingly — but he/she sees it all as such, also accordingly. This is Awareness on the March, as opposed to Awareness at Rest, or Shakti and Brahman, if you will.

**"Why did Jesus teach about his 'Second Coming' in the sky, and the 'End of the world?' Was it all allegorical?"**

"In the Sky" means, in the Sky of Awareness, not in the earthly ether. The "end of the world" means the death of the unripe ego that assumes the illusory world (relativity) to be real once the soul awakens to Divine Reality — either in the body or beyond it.

**"I have been wondering if people who are attached to pain because of someone who hurt them, if they, in their deaths, go to that person's world and are forced to live with that unresolved pain until it is resolved?"**

Again this would be so if certain transformational practices were not engaged in, in order to "turn the tide," as it were. That is why just sitting around brooding on the past and thinking oneself to be a sinner is a complete waste of time. We must convince the Divine Mother that what She wrote about us in the book of karma at the time of our errors, can be erased by Her now or later — and it is sadhana that convinces Her thus. Put another way, karma cannot be worked out in the dream state, but has to be worked out on earth, while in the physical body. This is best done in that lifetime wherein karmas were created, else one has to take on another body to do so. Moreover, heaven is hardly the place to work out karmas, for the mind is focused on celestial enjoyments. But these pass and one is plunged back into the earth plane again. Hopefully the soul will recognize karmas, get a teacher early on, and expunge them right away; then live in freedom. Some Buddhist schools say that this is a 3-lifetime scenario; one to recognize karma, a second to do sadhana and work it out, and third to live a conscious life followed by a conscious "death."

**"Is there a literal interpretation to 'taking refuge in' someone?"**

Spiritually speaking, I do not think there is a non-literal way of accomplishing that. A high ideal is beckoning to people all the time, but many do not recognize it, or it does not occur to them that this is what they are supposed to do. Put another way, they take refuge in their egos under the pretense of "I know what is best for me," but the ego is lost half of the time, and headed down a wrong track the other half. False humility and arrogance, respectively. are the two results of this wrong interpretation.

**"This world is maya, and all is ultimately Self, but I'm wondering from the perspective of reincarnation, could the people I 'hurt' in my dreams be related to a past life or unresolved karma?"**

Yes, and the karmas of the collective mind as well. It is so thick and impenetrable that seers advise that we transcend collective mind. This is good advice, for later, when perfection has been gained, we can return and help those same individuals, enmasse. Otherwise, it is all "the blind leading the blind," as they say, or, you are a part of the problems you are attempting to solve — i.e., you are in your own way, and a hindrance to those you are actually attempting to assist.

**"Could entities be 'taking refuge' in me, for better or worse?"**

Not consciously. For that to happen, one has to be free of one's own ignorance. Otherwise, it is all a rather random game of coming and going, only involving a pallid imitation of the rights, then wrongs, of everybody else, in cycles.

**"How can it be that the soul is carried along the nadis via prana, when nature is in the soul? How can the soul move when akasha is in the soul?"**

The soul, with a small "s" rather than a capitol "S," moves; the Atman, the real Soul, does not. That same soul, called the mind, as a complex of thought, intelligence, and ego, gets carried along nadis, subtle nerves, to whatever destination awaits it, according to its karmas. The main point of spiritual life and realization is to stop the soul's dream movements from occurring, and to thereby rest in the original static "position" which is Brahman. A being who can accomplish that is free of karmas, and will never create them again. Any embodiment such a Soul undertakes is on purpose, conscious, and for a great purpose, usually only known to Itself.

**"I understand that one should meditate without expectation. And one should love God for the sake of loving God. Without expectation. Like that unconditional love. However; how do you love something you can't feel? And when you look at a picture of God, be it in the form of Ramakrishna, Mother, or what have you, doesn't one feel love? IF you know God?"**

Instead of regretting that you cannot love what you cannot see or feel, try thinking about how, all your life, you loved everything here on earth that you could feel and see, and little ever came of it. Learn to love the formless Essence; it is far less problematic

**"How do we master desire? Granted I know it's a process. A long process. However, why is it that when I was meditating earlier I only felt Mother for about 2 weeks, and She disappeared. Then I felt the horrors of her leaving me. I don't remember what it felt like as its been years since that happened. And yet am I supposed to love God, not to be at peace but to love God for the sake of loving God."**

Just as you feel you do not want to be here in the body, on earth, so too do the illumined souls feel that way. Why should They come here? For, when they do come, they suffer too. So why do you call abandonment what is only natural to them, i.e., remaining close to God, Formlessness? Now, if you want to be like Them/near Them, meditate on the highest Brahman and pray to the Highest Ishvara. It is a waste of time to blame Them for our own inabilities. If anything, we ought to feel great happiness that They do not have to be here anymore. As Swamiji said, do not drag Divinity down to earth; raise yourself up and inwards to Divinity.

**"If I desire to love God, how does this come about if I don't know him. It's like telling me that John Doe from Asia left a picture here, and all of a sudden I am to love John Doe — although I don't see, hear, or feel John Doe. Of course I want to meditate and empty the mind at some point, but how do I if I'm not to force meditation? I try and sit for 15 minutes in the morning, but I get up because I just don't know why. Yet I am at the center every Sunday and able to sit for 1/2 hour, then 10 minutes."**

God in form came to you here on earth in the form of your Guru, and he told you about the Lord and Mother of all the devotees. You did not need to see Them; you heard about Them. That – The Word – started you on your path. I do not know about John Doe, but I do know that John the Apostle said that Jesus told him, "No man hath seen God with these eyes." So use your ears. God, Brahman, is both vibration and nonvibration. With your ears open and your eyes shut, you will hear Divine Reality speaking inside of you, and humming there. That Sound is Sight. Be still for hours at a time and listen.

**"Why is peace in the three worlds important for successful meditation?"**

Peace of mind is crucial for meditation in any world, and at all times. Simply put, there is no spiritual progress to be had via the lazy or restless mind. Though obviously apparent when spoken or written out like this, it is surprising how many beings go ahead and try to attain higher things – wisdom, worship, meditation, service – despite the presence of a restless mind. They need to work out their erratic tendencies first, then strive for the overall equanimity that is conducive to unbroken peace of mind. They also need a teacher to instruct them is this endeavor, but most will not take one. They try out conventional methods instead, attempting to use these as tools to achieve the higher ends of spiritual life. It will not work. As my teacher once said, *"The guru is not popular here in the West, and that is because the church has taken his place."* And what has the church ever done for spirituality other than to try and stamp it out? The way of religion is the way to heaven. The way of spirituality is the way to Enlightenment.

Even a peaceful mind does not guarantee spiritual growth right away. Those three elements that Holy Mother has cited, i.e., patience, purity, and perseverance must also play into the greater picture. This is due to the many subtle impressions that the mind holds, carelessly gathered and stored in previous lifetimes, that were not neutralized before the time of one's passing. Now, here they are again, springing up in this lifetime to spoil one's bid for said peace of mind.

Practical Vedantists do not expect that peace of mind will ever come to the three worlds. The opposite called, war, and the lack of peace of mind in most beings, stand against it. But striving for it, nonetheless, provides a good example and worthy goal for those looking on, so that pockets of peace may be extended, and war and restlessness be put off and reduced as far as possible.

**"What is the ultimate origin of desire or attachment?"**

The final answer, according to the radical nondual school of Advaita, is that everything is originless. Good or bad, higher or lower, there is no beginning, middle, or end to any of it. God, Nature, Human Beings, and Maya are all free of origin. By settling this question first, then one can look into the relative and apparent origins of things. It would help to be able to "count to five" for that search, because every set of fives (like the five elements) rolls out of another set of fives. But that is a subject for another set of questions. To focus on Ajativada, nonorigination, will clear that wash of conflicting questions around relativity from the mind, and leave all that is cosmological and philosophical by nature free to reveal itself. Then, "Come sweet khyati (clarity), come."

**"I have been reading on maya in your books. Since all is maya, perhaps the best way to look at maya is from the point of view of the realized individual, eg., Ramakrishna. He certainly lived in the world (maya) but was evidently free of it. How do you explain this? Some of the common statements are: 'the world is illusion,' or 'unreal.' These need to be clarified. He ate food, drank water, used transportation, lived in a temple; all maya? So in that sense maya is real. Is not maya all of creation?"**

Clarification comes when we define the world "unreal." Vedanta does not mean the world is unreal as in the cases of "water in a mirage," or "the son of a barren woman." These are metaphors (*abhavapadarthas*) used as examples for impossible things. Unreal in Vedanta means changing, thus *ultimately* unreal. That is, when the world goes away (like in deep sleep, death, a good meditation, and nondual samadhi) Reality, Brahman, remains. *"The one remains the same; the many change and pass."* Otherwise, nothing and no one — including maya — would come back. Something, such as yourself and nature, cannot be produced out of nothing. The eternal backdrop is always present, though never seen. Maya goes away with Liberation, but Brahman is the very nature of liberation.

As was just written above, Sri Ramakrishna — the real Paramahamsa, free of impurities — demonstrated how to live in the world but not be of it. *"The mud fish lives in the mud at the bottom of the lake, but its scales still shine." "The turtle swims in the boundless ocean joyfully, but its attentions lie on its eggs buried in the sand on the beach." "The duck gets into the water, but the water never gets into the duck." "The maidservant employed in the city takes care of the Master's children as if they were her own, but her mind dwells on her own children back at her home in the countryside." "Keep the boat in the water, but do not let water in the boat."* In so many simple but direct ways did the Great Master tell the people of the world about the risks and dangers of worldly life, while also informing them of a higher way to both deal with them and transform them.

**"How can it be that the soul is carried along the nadis via prana, when nature is in the soul? How can the soul move when akasha is in the soul?"**

The soul, with a small "s" rather than a capitol "S," moves; the Atman, the real Soul, does not. That same soul, called the mind, as a complex of thought, intelligence, and ego, gets carried along nadis, subtle nerves, to whatever destination awaits it, according to its karmas. The main point of spiritual life and realization is to stop the soul's dream movements from occurring, and to thereby rest in the original static "position" which is Brahman. A being who can accomplish that is free of karmas, and will never create them again. Any embodiment such a Soul undertakes is on purpose, conscious, and for a great purpose, usually only known to Itself.

It is in this way that we understand the distinction between the mental complex called a transmigrating "soul," and a stable, static, and all-pervasive Entity termed the "Soul," i.e., Atman. Peace belongs to That, and to nothing else.....

**"Sometimes you assert what sounds to me like a course of heroic willing, that if God's grace is not forthcoming, then get to enlightenment yourself; don't wait for God's grace, and blast your own karma. At other times you point out that the limitations on free will are so extreme, that it's almost as if there is no such thing. This can leave me feeling like the figure in Hindu mythology named Trishanku, who hangs suspended between Heaven and Earth and can neither go up nor down. Will you please harmonize these two poles of teaching?"**

My guru always used to say that Grace and Self-effort must go hand in hand, like the two wings of the bird. Holy Mother taught him that without engaging in self-effort, God's Grace will remain far away due to the mind's still present and persisting veils. Sri Ramakrishna taught Her that the wind of grace is always blowing, but that the spiritual mariner has to raise their sails to catch it. What is not wanted in this seeming dichotomy, is for any type of stunned state to occur to the mind, causing it to seek neither just because both represent two possibilities. Using present day mantras again, "Just do it" applies here. Once one is launched into sadhana, God's grace will show up as inherent spirituality — *"which was incomprehensible earlier due to the limitations of their own intellects,"* to quote the *Svetasvataropanisad*. To put it simply, all limitations are removed by sadhana. Grace is the natural result.

**"Can one equate psychic prana with Kundalini Shakti?"**

No, not equate, but connect. Kundalini Shakti is innately intelligent, supremely independent, and fully Aware. Prana, of all types — gross, subtle, psychic — is insentient, dependent on other forces, and unaware of itself. Prana has been likened to the web of a spider, and Kundalini to the spider herself. And the nadis through which her prana flows are actually quite weblike, yes? Through them She is in touch with everything, throughout all of creation. Ida, pingala, and sushumna are the three main strands of that vast web, connected back in to the Trinity. And thousands of tiny channels come off of them.

---

Questions, observations and insights regarding problems in spiritual life or the issues of the day may be directed to Nectar's editorial staff at srvinfo@srv.org and will be duly addressed in succeeding issues.

◆ *Rabbi Rami Shapiro*

# Learning to Live Under Water
## A Deeper Take on Happiness

I've been a Jew for 70 years. In all that time I never heard Jews talk about being happy. We talk about health a lot. And who hates us now. And Israel. But happiness? Never. Yet the Gallup Company's on–going survey of wellbeing in America shows that Jews are the happiest Americans alive today. I add the "alive today" just to be thorough. Perhaps dead people in heaven are happier than living Jews in America, but we have no data on that, so I don't want to speculate.

One odd finding is that while religious Jews are happier than religious Protestants [72.4% to 68.9%] nonreligious Jews, which means most Jews, are only one tenth of a percentage point less happy than the most religious Protestants: 68.9% for Protestants, 68.8% for Jews. Numbers aside, I just don't get it.

My Protestant neighbors are always praising Jesus and thanking God for all kinds of good things, while my Jewish family and friends always seem to be waiting for the next shoe to drop. Not just the other shoe as if there were only two to worry about, but the next one as if sorrow's closest was stocked with former First Lady of the Philippines, Imelda Marcos' 3000-plus shoe collection. For the Protestants I know things will always get better, if not in this world then the next. For Jews, on the other hand, it could always get worse.

I doubt that this outlook on life is what gets Jews to the top of the Gallup poll. Maybe we should look to the Bible for guidance.

### Outlook of the Hebrew Bible

The Hebrew Bible, however, rarely speaks of happiness, but when it does it offers some fairly practical advice. For example, in the Book of Deuteronomy a newly married soldier is exempted from any military service for one year so that he may *"give happiness to the woman he has married"* (Deuteronomy 24:5). Notice that happiness here is a euphemism for sexual pleasure and belongs to the wife rather than the husband, suggesting that for the author of Deuteronomy, men prefer to make war not love.

Things seem to change over the next 300 or 400 years so that by the time of Ecclesiastes while happiness is still linked to being with a woman, the pleasure is now mutual: *"Enjoy happiness with a woman you love all the fleeting days of your life, for that alone is what you can get out of life"* (Ecclesiastes 9:9).

Beyond the joy of sex, Ecclesiastes lays out a broader sense of what brings us happiness: sufficient food and drink (Ecclesiastes 2:24; 3:13; 5:17), meaningful work (Ecclesiastes 3:22), and one or two good friends upon whom one can rely in difficult times (Ecclesiastes 4:9–12). While Ecclesiastes is writing about individuals and not society as a whole, we can extrapolate from the text and argue that a society that promotes happiness is one that provides all its citizens with fair and equitable opportunities to secure food, drink, work, and marital and social bonds.

One could almost sum up the Biblical view of happiness by quoting the title of Elizabeth Gilbert's book, *Eat, Pray, Love*, except that "pray" is conspicuously absent from the Bible's formula for happiness. Nowhere in the Hebrew Bible is one told to pray for happiness, or that prayer will make you happy. On the contrary, God seems to be irrelevant when it comes to happiness.

### Job's Complain About the Wicked

*"They spend their days in happiness and go down to Sheol (the netherworld) in peace. They say to God, 'Leave us alone. We don't want to learn Your ways. Why should we serve You? What benefit is gained by praying to You?'* (Job 21:13–14).

> "Nowhere in the Hebrew Bible is one told to pray for happiness, or that prayer will make you happy. On the contrary, God seems to be irrelevant when it comes to happiness."

Job goes on to say that there is no real difference in the fate of the righteous and the wicked, and happiness is arbitrary: *"One person dies wealthy and unburdened by disease, tranquil and at peace; another dies embittered, never having tasted a moment's happiness. Yet they both die, they both are buried, and they both are given over to worms"* (Job 21: 23–26).

Job's attitude probably explains why Jews are by and large uninterested in happiness and the afterlife.

I realize of course that most beings are not Jewish, and that most are interested in getting into Heaven, or Nirvana, or some other state of consciousness where one may imagine endless happiness is to be found. For the sake of such perspectives, let me take a slight detour and provide you with the keys to Heaven.

### One Essential Question for Heaven-Seekers

At the end of tractate *Kiddushin* of the Palestinian *Talmud* we are taught that when you die you will be asked only one question, the answer to which will determine whether or not you get to enter Heaven: *"Why did you not partake of every legitimate pleasure life provided?"* Or, to put it more simply, why did you postpone happiness? You were made for pleasure. You were made to be happy. And life was given to you for this purpose. Lucky for us we are still alive. Luckier still we now know God's primary question. So, go, enjoy, be happy!

**The Secret to Exquisite Enjoyment**

But how? How can you set yourself up each day to partake of the legitimate pleasures life lays out before you? One answer is the recitation of a Hebrew mantra called *Shiviti*, "I have placed." The full mantra is "*Shviti YHVH l'negdi tamid: I place the Divine before me, always.*" The purpose of the mantra is to awaken you to the Divine in, with, and as all reality. Read Rabbi Levi Yitzchak of Berdichev's (1740–1810) poetic expression of this:

the earth and wipe humanity off the face of the planet. And he plans to do so in thirty minutes! God sends the four of them back to their respective peoples to prepare them for their impending doom.

The priest goes back to his flock and urges everyone to confess their sins and prepare for the end with Last Rites. The minister goes back to her community and urges her people to open their hearts to Christ that they may be welcomed into heaven when they die. The imam calls his community together and urges that the people pray and affirm the infinite mercy and compassion of Allah. The rabbi also returns and gathers the Jews into the synagogue. After explaining the situation, he says, "Alright. We have thirty minutes to learn how to live under water!"

> "How can you set yourself up each day to partake of the legitimate pleasures life lays out before you? One answer is the recitation of a Hebrew mantra called *Shiviti*, 'I have placed.' The full mantra is '*Shviti YHVH l'negdi tamid: I place the Divine before me, always.*' The purpose of the mantra is to awaken you to the Divine in, with, and as all reality."

*Where can I find You—and where can I not find You?*
*Above—only You;*
*Below—only You;*
*To the east—only You;*
*To the west—only You;*
*To the south—only You;*
*To the north—only You;*
*If it is good—it is You;*
*If it is not—also You;*
*It is You; it is always only You.*

This is not easy or even pleasant. God is reality, and reality isn't all sugar and spice. In Isaiah 45:7, God tells us that God alone forms light and dark, good and evil. In Deuteronomy 30:19 we learn that God places before us birthing and dying, blessing and cursing, and urges us to choose life despite the fact that life contains all these things. In other words, God, reality itself, isn't always to our liking, and yet we can still be happy if we learn to love what is, just *as it is*.

This is what Job urges us to do when he says to his wife in the face of terrible tragedy, "*Should we not accept the bad as well as the good from God*" *(Job 2:9)*. We should accept it all, and when we do, we know that it is all from God and indeed is God, and this realization is the key to whatever happiness we may find by noticing and engaging with the legitimate pleasures that may be found even in the greater sadnesses in life.

**An Interesting Story**

A rabbi, a priest, a minister, and an imam are called to heaven to meet with God. When they arrive, they are told that despite promises to the contrary, God plans once again to flood

Rabbi Rami Shapiro is an award-winning author, poet, essayist, and educator whose poems have been anthologized in over a dozen volumes, and whose prayers are used in prayer books around the world. Rami received rabbinical ordination from the Hebrew Union College–Jewish Institute of Religion and holds doctoral degrees in both Jewish studies and divinity. A congregational rabbi for 20 years, Rabbi Shapiro currently teaches Religious Studies at Middle Tennessee State University, and directs One River (**www.one-river.org**), a not-for-profit educational foundation devoted to building community through contemplative conversation. Rami writes a regular column for Spirituality and Health Magazine called Roadside Assistance on Your Spiritual Journey. His most recent books are The Sacred Art of Lovingkindness, The Divine Feminine, and Open Secrets from which this essay was adapted. Rabbi Rami can be reached through his website, **www.rabbirami.com**

◆ *Babaji Bob Kindler*

# THE TRIPLE GEM OF VEDANTA
## Cosmology, Practice, and Nonduality — in One Path

Though Mother India has many paths, sampradayas, darshanas, and sects, the "triple gem" gracing the Divine Goddess' central ring finger is the precious jeweled ornament of Sankhya, Yoga, and Vedanta. How beautiful its appearance, how radiant its sheen, how illuminating its luster. Swami Vivekananda likened it to the body, energy, and head of true Religion, all combined. Taking it up, the ardent aspirant of today will easily put to rest all uncertainties around religion, all questions about philosophy, and all doubts and fears of the struggling mind in relativity — in maya. However, even many practitioners of Vedanta today are unaware of the import, as well as the role, of this powerful threefold package — of all that led up to the Vedantic period around Vedavyasa's time.

### Sankhya Very Much, Lord Kapila!

At the time of the appearance of Sankhya Yoga and its famous list of twenty-four cosmic principles (tattvas), a foundational system that is attributed to Lord Kapila, India still had to see and welcome the coming of Sri Krishna, the Dvapara Yuga Avatar. Modern speculations, based upon the recent discovery of the battlefield upon which the war between the Kauravas and Pandavas took place, puts Lord Krishna's birth approximately around 2500 years B.C.E. In the Bhagavad Gita, Sri Krishna states, "....of sages, I am Kapila." So the ancient birth of Lord Kapila was much earlier.

Whatever the case may be, most all of India's systems of worship, practice, and wisdom, took a huge clue and key from Lord Kapila's Sankhya Yoga philosophy, and proceeded to build and expand upon it, each in their own times. As they did, they left its basic tenets and their philosophical premises untouched — out of great reverence. Thus, as a philosophy in its own right, it became the fundamental cosmology of India overall. With it in mind, the seeker after Enlightenment could readily trace the way back through the many layers of manifestation through endless cycles of time, arriving at the ultimate Source. This was accomplished via following each tattva and connecting it to its previous origin, like earth to the sense of smell, water to the sense of taste, fire to the sense of sight, etc. This revealed an inner staircase that the involving soul utilized, step by step, to go deeper towards the Source, or Brahman.

Lord Kapila

### Father of Yoga Many Times Over

At the time when Patanjali composed his Eight-limbed system of Yoga called Patanjala, or Raja Yoga, somewhere around 200-300 A.D., he guided practitioners to use the twenty-four tattvas of Sankhya as stations for meditation, calling them "*alambanas.*" Each was to be contemplated on its own merit, in different ways as guided by the spiritual preceptor. When they were understood to be both insentient, and projected by the mind (at cosmic, collective, and individual levels), their ability to impede the seeker due to attachment to them fell away, they being purified in the fire of Jnanam turned white-hot by Dhyanam (dharmic wisdom and meditation). The attainment of the higher limbs of Yoga was thus facilitated, bringing the lost soul back from the confusion of ages and embedding it soundly in the firmament of living Intelligence.

Patanjali

### Mother India's Most Mature Child

As the centuries progressed, and the thinking process of many beings remained both superficial and darksome, the darshana of Vedanta matured and took hold. Vedavyasa, affectionally called "The Father of Vedanta," was said to have lived somewhere between 500 BCE and 400 CE, but some historians say that his famous commentary on Patanjali's Eight-limbed Yoga occurred around 500 CE. Some historians and scholars place the general date of Vedavyasa's birth more like 1500 BCE, and Patanjali's about 500 BCE. Whatever the case, and because these souls took bodies consciously throughout centuries in order to keep the teachings alive in the world, only a general timeline can be formulated.

More importantly, great lights showed up in the sweep of the Vedantic period, such as the advaitic luminaries Gaudapada and Shankara. For such as these, and given the thickness of ignorance that had set in despite Lord Buddha (550 B.C.) and Patanjali (200 A.D.) having been on the world scene, the emphasis around the twenty-four cosmic principles shifted towards the challenge and ability to dissolve them all via disidentification with all of matter. The great practice of *Neti Neti*, "I am not this, not this," gave the order or permission to serious practitioners to detach and transcend all the tattvas, placing the focus upon merging the radiant and unbound leftover "Self" called Atman into the highest and deepest state of nondual Awareness. As Shankara wrote in his *Vivekachudamani*, "*The practitioner of blissful dissolution merges the word into the mind, the mind into the intellect, the intellect into the ego, the ego into the Witness, the Witness into Atman, and Atman into Brahman. Brahman is the Soul of All. In this way does the masterful seeker gain eternal peace and unalloyed bliss.*"

Vedavyasa

In all these three phases of fine philosophy (see chart on facing page) — Sankhya as cosmology, Yoga as practice, and Vedanta as nonduality — both close association and intrinsic

# The Three Great Philosophical Footfalls of India

*"Centuries and millennia will come and go as India's sacred philosophical systems dissolve and re-emerge continually, but these quantum leaps in spans of time never erode the intrinsic connections that bind these eternal darshanas fast into one, inseparable, and indestructible Truth-principle."*
— *Babaji Bob Kindler*

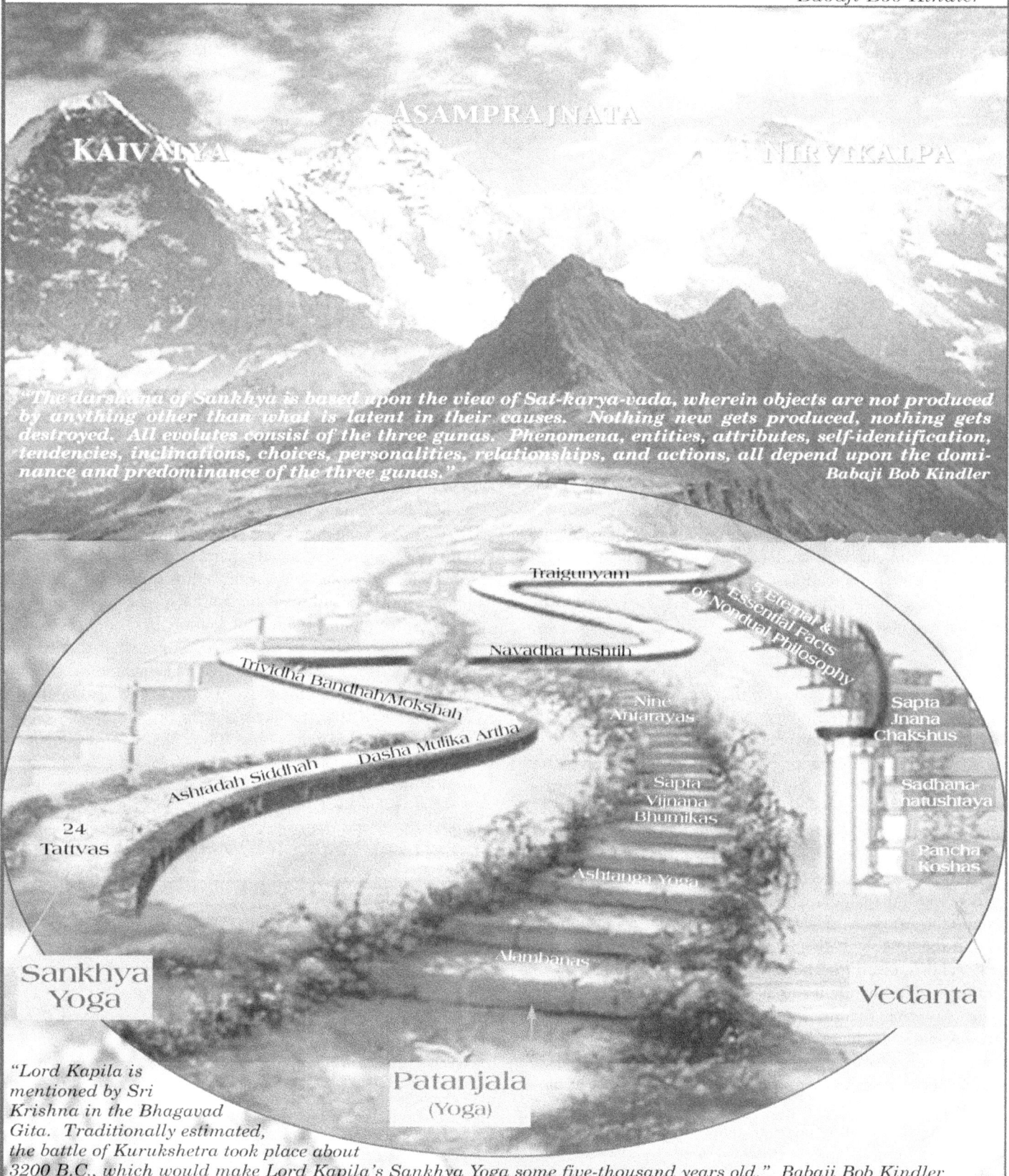

*"The darshana of Sankhya is based upon the view of Sat-karya-vada, wherein objects are not produced by anything other than what is latent in their causes. Nothing new gets produced, nothing gets destroyed. All evolutes consist of the three gunas. Phenomena, entities, attributes, self-identification, tendencies, inclinations, choices, personalities, relationships, and actions, all depend upon the dominance and predominance of the three gunas."*
— *Babaji Bob Kindler*

*"Lord Kapila is mentioned by Sri Krishna in the Bhagavad Gita. Traditionally estimated, the battle of Kurukshetra took place about 3200 B.C., which would make Lord Kapila's Sankhya Yoga some five-thousand years old."* — *Babaji Bob Kindler*

connection wove the turning of ages together. Truth, like magma flowing from the summit of a volcano to the shores far below via a protective lava tube, was able to reach present times, even find its way to materialistic America thanks to the universal mind and spirit of Swami Vivekananda.

Of course (and as the chart on the previous page reveals) the cosmic principles — whether seen as limiting superimpositions to dissolve (upadhis), as stations of projected thought for meditating upon (alambanas), or steps of a cosmic stairway that can return the sojourning soul to its Source, were only a part of the greater picture, a sort of Sankhya/Yoga/Vedanta 101 teaching. Sankhya's aim and end was *Kaivalya*; Yoga's was *Asamprajnata Samadhi*; and Vedanta's has always been *Nirvikalpa Samadhi*. All of Mother India's spiritual pathways court Formlessness, including Buddhism with its *Nirvana*, and ultimately, Tantra, with its *Mahayoga*.

Vivekananda

### Gems of Inestimable Value, like the Pearl of Great Price

This precious triple gem is not earned or easily possessed, either. Self-effort, daily practice, spiritual discipline, sadhana — these are names for what is required to attain to such lofty heights of authentic spirituality. An easy, comfortable, conventional religious path is relatively useless in procuring the enlightenment that these Indian darshanas can confer, particularly when they are well-guided by an acharya. Such lukewarm religion cannot set the seeker up for even approaching the early stages of comprehension of nonduality and its import. There must be intense participation in one's own attempt towards gaining freedom. This is why great souls take to these exceptional spiritual avenues lifetime after lifetime — if they take on a body at all.

As the chart displayed in this article illustrates, all three paths are lavishly decorated with supporting concomitants. Sankhya has its cautionary *Navadha Tushtih*, the Nine Complacencies, that unfortunately occupy the minds of beginning and intermediate practitioners. A short summation of these would be that many seekers, though they may listen to instructions from advanced teachers, nevertheless still secretly, even subconsciously, rely upon such misleading elements of worldly life as matter, time, destiny, luck, and wealth as their real motivators. All of these are to be renounced, plain and simple if Freedom is desired. Therefore, Sankhya also places in the foreground the *Astadhah Siddhah*, the Eight Great Accomplishments, so that the aspirant knows for certain where to concentrate his or her efforts, i.e., transcending the three types of suffering while gaining such authentic boons as making the spiritual path one's own, mastering the study of scriptures, attaining the eternal friendship of an enlightened guru and a supportive sangha — all for the purpose of securing a pure mind. With all of these in hand, the transcendence of the three gunas — *Traigunyam* — will be possible.

In Yoga, the attainment of samadhi is the aim, and so Patanjali splits the topic into two — seeded and unseeded — then maps out the seeded into four subdivisions. There are seven stages of knowledge that are gained along the way as well, called the *Sapta Jnana Bhumikas*. These are termed *Sapta Jnana Chakshus* in Vedanta, that has seven *ajnana bhumikas* as well, which are lower states of knowledge that the ignorant and sleeping soul has still to navigate and transcend.

In Vedanta, however, the *Sadhanachatushtaya* is all the rage, also called the "Four Treasures and Six Jewels." It is a purely mental/intellectual practice, meant for mastery by advanced seekers. These are more of attainments than they are practices, and possess all the powerful elements in them to destroy the final vestiges of root ignorance and lift the soul majestically to a perfectly realized state. Here, Vedanta's statement of what is, and Yoga's insistence on what must be, is a consummate coupling. In all of this, as well, the Wisdom Mother's secret hand is at work, as always. In commenting on Lord Patanjali's Yoga Sutras, Vedavyasa cites the import of the Divine Mother's timely assistance in this crucial process, stating, *Purusham artham shunyanam gunayam prati pravashah kaivalya svarupa pratistha va chitti-shaktih iti*, which translates as: *"That primal shakti power, who involves transmigrating consciousness back to its Source, and who strips nature of all name and form in the interim, accomplishes both, so that the soul can attain to its final Liberation."*

### One Unbroken Religious Stream

In this day and age it is hard to imagine, but easy to envision, that the Semitic religions really form one, cohesive flow of divine awareness. From Abraham, to Moses, to Jesus, to Mohammed, all is one; it was really only mankind that split them asunder. In India, with its penchant for successfully bringing all factions into alignment and integration by always perceiving them so, naturally, all the various darshanas that formed over ages got nourished by the expansive and ongoing insights and realizations of one another. Rishis like Kapila, Patanjali, and Vedavyasa, with their precious systems of Sankhya, Yoga, and Vedanta, prove this point, obviously. Among other important features, they also demonstrate to the world what India's serious practice of *ahimsa*, nonviolence, can accomplish — not just in the area of human relations, but also in the realm of the deepest devotional yearning for God, and the loftiest philosophical thought leading to Nonduality.

Babaji Bob Kindler is the Spiritual Director of the SRV Associations with its two centers in Hawaii and Oregon. A teacher of religion and spirituality and a prolific author, his books include *The Avadhut, Twenty-Four Aspects of Mother Kali, Ten Divine Articles of Sri Durga, Swami Vivekananda Vijnanagita, Sri Sarada Vijnanagita, An Extensive Anthology of Sri Ramakrishna's Stories, A Quintessential Yoga Vasishtha, Reclaiming Kundalini Yoga, Footfalls of the Indian Rishis, and others*. Founder and Artistic Director of Jai Ma Music, he is also an accomplished musician and composer who has produced over twenty-five albums of instrumental and devotional music to date.

# The Three Blind Men and the Elephant
## Ego/Nonego as a Characteristic of the Present Moment

Non-dual truth was presented to me with the story of an elephant and three blind people. One blind person describes the trunk as a hose. Another describes the tail as a snake, and the third a leg as a tree. The metaphor suggests our limited perspective is the reason God is explained in different ways. The metaphor evoked a response, "I don't believe that."

**My Leg is the Elephant, and Your Tail is Wrong**

My response was caused by several considerations. It was not based on an exclusive handle on the truth. As a chaplain I have often been confronted with definitive claims that my leg or trunk is the whole elephant. Or that my trunk is definitive, and your leg is misguided. Tearing off a leg to beat on someone who has a hold of the trunk is one of the grim lessons of history. What starts as interfaith dialogue can devolve to interfaith rivalry. This is true especially in prisons where race-based identification and gang related behavior can be couched in religion. Exclusive religious claims can result in elephant dissection or contention.

**I Understand More about my Leg by Trying to Understand your Handle on a Tail**

My grasp of the elephant is informed by many contributing personal and historical factors. Some of these sources I shared in Nectar of Nondual Truth, Issue #34, in a short contribution that was titled, *Interfaith Reflections*. The elements that compose my hold on the elephant's anatomy amount to a culmination of influences. My worldview is influenced by things like "middle class, Presbyterian, West Coast, prison chaplain, theologically trained." Mentors, friends, personal reflection, and devotional study, continue to refine my understanding of the hold I have of the elephant. I consider myself a practicing adherent of Christianity.

Life experience has afforded me the opportunity to encounter a variety of religious traditions and study some philosophy. To acknowledge evolving worldviews is part of how I make sense of things. These forms of specific life experience inform my perspective. I encounter perspectives from others that refine or transform my own. A dialectical character to experience creates a dynamic of transformation because of the differing parts of the elephant. My response to the story of the elephant and its parts is nuanced by a commitment to pluralism in culture and dualism in philosophy.

**I Have Hold of a Snake**

I presume an existence and this perspective is a function of ego. Ego is coincident with personal experience. Ego is a point of reference intrinsic to experience, and others share a perspective on the world that appears like my own. The experience of ego is similar in an abstract way, because of the different circumstances that surround everyone. Our grasp upon the differing parts of the elephant have qualities that are both complementary and mutually exclusive. A discussion of universalism should be able to contain the problem of personal differences consistent with varying circumstances, and the specificity of how the present moment is experienced. We exist coincident with factors such as our education, family of origin, historical period, cultural and intellectual influences. These factors are intrinsic to our perception of the elephant. Our self-understanding is malleable, and contingent on these factors.

There are also qualitative differences that typify experience. The experience of a monastery as opposed to a boot camp invites a different response because of different settings. An individual's response to a circumstance or setting also appears to differ substantially. For example, being loving, hateful, resentful, or contrite are qualitative differences that affect how the present moment is experienced. Accrued experience and the consequences ascribed to an individual's accomplishments also have the nature of being distinct. Universal truth must contain the multiplicity that characterizes personal experience. The elephant can be posited as an amalgamation of its parts, but even if I had a hold of a tail, and thought it was a snake, it could appear to me to be the elephant.

**This Reminds me of a Tree**

The hold I have on reality is a construct. A hold on reality is subjective and determined in part by associations with past experiences. Not only do we form subjective constructs, but the objects or external reality to which we relate truncates and defines us. Reciprocity is the foundation of experience. The experience of a dynamic to consciousness duly reflects this reciprocity.

The holder and that which is held is foundational in both an epistemological and a phenomenological sense. The contradictions posed by tails and trunks, and the fluid relatedness of the holder and the held, presents a paradoxical and mutually negating foundation to experience. These dichotomies become absolute, not just linguistically, but are determinate in an existential sense. We are defined or expressive of these circumstances as they are identified. The reciprocity of the seer and the seen, subjective awareness and objective circumstance, historical encounter and transtemporal insight, characterize an experience of self. In terms of a subjective self positively identifying a self or ego, we could state, "I have hold of a tree" and also "the tree produces me." What we experience is a fluid capacity of awareness that is objectified, and is reified by the objects it lights upon.

this essay, the influence that the Kyoto School Philosophy and Masao Abe exerted became clear to me. My clerk at the prison where I was a chaplain helped refine my thoughts.

A dynamic process of transformation is intrinsic to the his-

> "The religious experiences of mystics or saints of different traditions are similar. The virtuous character traits of those accomplished in spirituality across the world are also essentially identical. We look to these similarities as an affirmation of universal religious truth. I value the solidarity, affection, and intent that form common bonds between people of different traditions."

Time is a function of experience. A historical sense provides a growing edge to experience through a dynamic character of consciousness. Revelations of science, refinements of culture, creative new forms in art, manufacturing, societal values, and many other factors conspire to assist in manifesting this growing edge. We personalize these factors as "my life," "our time of history," or "my people." This tendency to personalize experience complements this growing edge that has been created by the contributing factors of a fluid, evolving quality to our experience. We define and understand an ego through the many contributing forms of awareness experienced as this growing edge of the present.

### My Leg and Your Tail Are More Alike Than Different

The religious experiences of mystics or saints of different traditions are similar. The virtuous character traits of those accomplished in spirituality across the world are also essentially identical. We look to these similarities as an affirmation of universal religious truth. I value the solidarity, affection, and intent that form common bonds between people of different traditions. Despite having a leg as compared to a trunk, we all appear to have hold of an elephant.

The content of spiritual realization finds expression in the historical and cultural nature of personal experience. The partial view of leg, tail, or trunk, is consistent with the self-expression of God. The elephant is created by its parts. The form of the elephant is a work in progress as the different characteristics of each part is experienced or revealed in time. I appreciate a creative tension between the whole and the parts. To posit a whole distinct from the elephant's parts is another type of elephant dissection.

### You Think It is a Snake, Mine Feels like a Tree

The parts of the elephant provide a vehicle for prompting new dimensions of understanding through the relationships between interrelated parts. New insight is encouraged by exploring the differences between legs and tails and trunks. Some specifically Eastern concepts have helped flesh out the part of the elephant I can grasp. For example, the rewarding experience of interfaith dialogue with the SRV gurus has helped me grow into a new understanding of time. In the process of producing

torical present. Consciousness evolves both individually and collectively through this process of differentiation and contrast. The idea of a theological purpose or intent is expressed through the process. This Universal Religious journal, *Nectar of Nondual Truth*, promotes this growing edge through these forms of dialectical philosophical reflection. Being asked to share my views is an honor.

### Your Leg is Different than My Tail

History presents evolving perspectives that takes form as polemics. Religious idealism as expressed by contemplative Christianity has given way to forms of materialism in much of contemporary Western religion. Literalism in Biblical scholarship and the historicity of the Biblical narrative are a common litmus test of orthodoxy within contemporary Christian practice. An ethos toward individualism and nationalism also appear to be on the rise.

The historicity of the Biblical narrative, scientism, and materialism, have supplanted previously more widely held worldviews characterized as philosophical idealism and contemplative spirituality. The empiricism of the Western philosophy has largely abandoned forms of idealism that had been more widely held in Western philosophical worldviews. Both the contemporary church and civic society in the United States reflects forms of polarization.

Western and Eastern theologies provide another form of dialectic in religious thinking, and there is currently a greater dissemination of eastern religions is the West. A characterization of religious perspectives could ascribe an exoteric empiricism of Western thought in contrast to an esoteric quality in Eastern religious thinking. Admittedly, this juxtaposition of East and West is stereotypical, but all these polemics exemplify how contrast allows for understanding to be refined. The empiricism of the West has been invigorated by a deeper capacity for self-refection through the teaching and insights of the Eastern traditions. The interpenetration of West and East helped provoke or integrate reflective capacities that have been languishing in Christian practice.

### This is Not a Snake, That is Not a Tree; but I Have Hold of Something

The understanding of God reflects polemics. Differentiating between the positive qualities of God or dispelling misunderstandings concerning the nature of God is represented by cataphatic and apophatic theologies. A similar polemic can be posited with Hinayana and Mahayana theologies in the East. Western and Eastern theologies provide another form of dialectic in religious thinking. Mutually exclusive, contradictory, paradoxical, and complementary patterns have been identified as the Hegelian Dialectic in contemporary philosophy. Such either/or differentiations do not sufficiently explain the qualities of God. This is particularly true when positing a polemic of empirical physical reality complemented by conscious self-reflection.

A simple juxtaposition of Creator/creation, East/West, conscious/unconscious, unity/multiplicity or subject/object reduces the many contributing qualifications of personal experience to a level of abstraction that is inconsistent with the intimate nature of personal experience and the evolving qualifications of the historical present. Upon reflection, I would say that the self-organization of consciousness is structured by polemics or dialectics, but these forms of duality cannot fully contain the nature of this self-expression.

### This Tree Seems to be Undergoing Some Type of Metamorphosis

The contemplative transcendence identified by Western mysticism offers insight into the most refined forms of contemplative idealism that sought to reconcile duality to a form of non-dual experience. The self-expression of Absolute Nothingness is a philosophical formulation that acknowledges that which transcends the categories of experience that are coincident of consciousness in Kyoto School Philosophy.

To identify that which is non-dual often abrogates normative forms of awareness or philosophical categories and the factors that color a personal context. The negation of the normative forms of awareness is termed Sunyata, Absolute Nothingness or the experience of Nothingness. More generally, mysticism gives expression to a non-dual foundation for identifying this non objectifiable characteristic. I understand that "deep sleep" simulates the non-dual experience in Vedanta.

Absolute Nothingness is a concept advanced by theologians through the Kyoto school of Buddhist philosophy. This insight resolves the polemic of something/nothing reflected in a dualistic approach to understanding the nature of the elephant. A radical detachment of subjective awareness or a form of oblivion does not adequately account for the dynamic nature of experience or the sense of personal agency consistent with experience. Oblivion is not the primary qualification most adepts, sages, or mystics ascribe to the experience.

Our religious and cultural heritages recognize extraordinary examples of those that shake our grip and advance new forms of awareness not dependent on the ego identification. Apophatic traditions posit formulas intrinsic to wresting our grip. The Kyoto School Philosophy emerged when Japanese Buddhist intellectuals of the Zen Buddhist tradition encountered Hegelian and Western philosophies. Western philosophical perspectives were assimilated and applied to Japanese forms of Buddhism. This provides an example of how a process of critical engagement and reflection gives rise to new insight. The deconstruction and assimilation of different perspectives transform our grasp of the elephant.

### Thanks for Asking About My Grasp of the Elephant

Informing the perspective of this essay is my background in mysticism and a form of idealism that provides an anti-thesis to the trending materialism of our times. A variety of devotional practices and relationships inspire me. Articulating this essay in the form of a dialectic was provoked by a set of circumstances. Admittedly, consciousness functions in ways I cannot understand, might be ubiquitous, or might not be dependent upon the epistemological observation of a perceiver and the perceived in the present moment. But I would contend that the present moment is nominally realized through a perceiver and the perceived, and in my experience is coincident with the many contributing qualifications of a place and time. The perspective I have sought to articulate is the consequence of factors not of my making, but am subject to or that happened to me. Individuals are coincident with the circumstances, history, and values that inform and truncate their expression in the world. The views I have sought to articulate are a product of particular circumstances.

My response to the story of the elephant required further elaboration. The amalgamation of parts falls short of adequately constructing a whole. I felt the need to also express the premise, "There is no non-dual truth," but not as a negation of a philosophical claim or to say there is no elephant, but as an affirmation of that which cannot be objectified.

Reverend Chris von Lobedan has served Shutter Creek Correctional Institution in Coos Bay Oregon for 17 years. His Doctor of Ministry and Master of Divinity were awarded from San Francisco Theological Seminary. He was the pastor of the First Presbyterian Church of Coos Bay for 13 years. He was recognized with the Transitional Services Employee of the Year award for his work in the religious reentry program Home for Good. He has worked extensively inside his institution to train volunteers to understand the importance of assisting those with whom they work with faith-based assistance as they transition from prison. He has brought a specific faith-traditions approach to that training and been one of the leaders in the development of Home for Good.

SWAMI BRAHMESHANANDA

# SATYA
## The Virtue of Truthfulness

The young Kauravas and Pandavas were learning their first lessons. The acharya pronounced the Vedic text: *Satyam vada, dharmam chara,* "*Speak the truth, follow the path of righteousness,*" and asked the pupils to repeat. Every one repeated. The teacher asked them to memorize the text. The next day he asked what they had learnt the previous day. All pronounced: *satyam vada, dharmam chara,* except Yudhishthira. Surprised, the acharya asked why could he, the eldest and the brightest among the one hundred and five pupils, not learn such a simple lesson? What Yudhishthira said in reply was an indication of his future greatness as the exemplar par-excellence of truth. He plainly confessed that he had not yet learnt to speak the truth. Others might have memorized the few words, but that certainly was not the purport of this short but profound precept: *satyam vada* — speak the truth. Unless one speaks the truth in day-to-day life, what use is it to merely memorize a few words? It took years of relentless practice and untold suffering for Yudhishthira to practice this precept in life — to truly learn that kindergarten lesson.

**Speak the Truth**

This is indeed the first moral lesson which a child learns on the lap of the mother, or from its teacher. In every civilized society truth is highly respected, and yet, in day-to-day life there is no other moral value which is more neglected than truth. The reason is that to observe truth is as difficult as it is easy to utter the word "truth."

According to Sri Ramakrishna, the observance of truth is the austerity most suited for, and efficacious in, the present Iron Age (*Kaliyuga*). The *Srimad Bhagavatam,* too, is of the opinion that of the four limbs of dharma, only one remains in *Kaliyuga,* and that is the observance of truth. Mahatma Gandhi, the greatest exponent and advocate of truth in modern times, goes a step further. He equates truth with God

Nothing is or exists in reality except Truth. That is why *sat,* or Truth, is perhaps the most important name of God. In fact, it is more correct to say that Truth is God, than to say that God is Truth.

Hence, according to Gandhi, none can attain to God without practicing truthfulness. And since he equates truth with God, he gives it precedence over other moral values, although according to Patanjali's Yoga Sutras, *Ahimsa,* non-violence, is the foremost value.

**Three Categories of Truth**

While truth, in the sense of Absolute Reality, may be the same as God, there is no way of knowing or experiencing it in our day-to-day life when we are confronted everywhere with what may be termed relative, empirical truth, or *vyàvahàrika satya,* conditioned by our mind and senses. If X is the reality and Y our mind, what we know is X+Y and never X. Let us take a few examples. The sky has no color, but it appears blue. The sun neither sets nor rises, and yet due to the rotation of the earth it appears to rise and set. Although the universe is made up of subatomic particles, to our limited vision it appears to be made up of gross elements and solid structures. Our social conduct is also influenced by our conditionings. A man is seen as a father by his son, as a son by his father, as a husband by his wife, as a brother by his brother, as a boss by his servant, as a subordinate by his boss, and so on. And yet, he is not only all these; he is also something more. The objects of the world are neither good nor bad, but we project our values on them and consider them either desirable, undesirable, or neutral.

There is a third category of reality, which may be termed apparent reality or, *pràtibhàsika satya.* A rope may appear as a snake in the dark; a piece of mother-of-pearl may appear like silver; water may appear to be present in a mirage, and so on. Dreams appear as real. These are only apparent realities. The goal of the practice of truthfulness is to attain to the Absolute Reality, *pàramàrthika satya,* by observing empirical, relative truth and by giving up the apparent truth.

**Sadhana: Practice**

Ideally, truthfulness must be practiced in its totality i.e., in thought, word, and deed. Truthfulness in deed consists in observing the code of conduct, injunctions and inhibitions of one's station in life. It also includes observance of vows and fulfillment of promises and resolves. Grandsire Bhishma's observance of the life-long vow of celibacy, and the observance of truth by king Harishchandra are a few of the brightest examples of truthful conduct. The observance of the vow of *pàtivratya* — faithfulness to the husband by a chaste wife — also falls under the same category.

A practitioner of truth must, however, begin by observing and acting according to his spoken word. A few examples from the life of Sri Ramakrishna and which he described himself, are illuminating:

*"If by chance I say that I will go to the pine-grove, I must go there even if there is no further need of it, lest I lose my attachment to truth."*

*"If once I say that I shall not eat, then it is impossible for me to eat, even if I am hungry. Again, if I ask a particular man to take my water jug to the pine-grove, he alone must carry it. If another man carries it, he will have to take it back."*

> "Often, during mental agitation and excitement, we may lose control over our speech and may start talking nonsense. Thus it is obvious that speaking truth is not easy and demands great self-control, carefulness, and alertness. It is wiser to be always on guard and speak only when required and no more than what is absolutely essential. *'No man can safely speak but he who loves silence.'*"

While this might be the technique to be followed by a beginner, the actual observance of truth consists in following one's conscience. Once Swami Adbhutananda was invited by a devotee for lunch. The swami accepted the invitation and promised to reach the devotee's house at the appointed hour. However, it started raining so heavily that the devotee assumed that the swami, in all probability, would not turn up. He was therefore surprised to see the Swami coming to his house at the appointed hour, wading through knee-deep water. When the devotee asked, 'Does truthfulness consist in keeping one's expressed word?' the swami replied:

*"Of course not. To observe truthfulness means so many things. Don't think that to act up to one's expressed words is all of truthfulness. It really means keeping one's resolve. That resolve may be expressed in words, or may be kept in the mind; and it might as well find expression in work leading ultimately to the fulfillment of the resolve which was never expressed in words. Have an understanding of the real ideal and having known it, stick to it under all circumstances and work for its realization. This is what is known as observance of truth, not merely keeping one's words. This Truth is God's power, God Himself."*

Mahatma Gandhi is also of the opinion that truthfulness consists in following one's conscience, and acting according to what one considers just and righteous, however difficult it might be. If truth were a bed of roses, everyone would follow it. We must stick to truth, even if the heavens were to fall, he would say.

**Spoken Truth**

According to the Bhagavad Gita, our speech must be truthful, agreeable, beneficial to all and must not cause any disturbance to the speaker or the listener. It is not advisable to speak an unpleasant truth nor a pleasant falsehood. Vyasa, in his commentary on Patanjali's Yoga Sutras, lays down certain conditions for truthful speech: (a) It must be according to what is heard, seen or inferred; (b) it must not be deceitful or meaningless to the listener and (c) it must be beneficial and not harmful. It is obvious that these conditions cannot be easily fulfilled. One must, therefore, be very careful in his speech. Sri Ramakrishna did not approve of a lie spoken even in a joke. He once took Rakhal, his favorite disciple, to task for speaking a lie jokingly. One may likewise speak an untruth prompted by greed, fear, or delusion. Peter, the foremost disciple of Jesus Christ, lied out of fear and denied thrice that he was Christ's disciple. Often, during mental agitation and excitement, we may lose control over our speech and may start talking nonsense. Thus it is obvious that speaking truth is not easy and demands great self-control, carefulness, and alertness. It is wiser to be always on guard and speak only when required and no more than what is absolutely essential. *"No man can safely speak but he who loves silence."*

While it may be difficult to adhere so strictly to truth always, especially for householders, they must at least avoid cheating others, giving false evidence in or out of the court of law, forging documents, etc. This is the second condition laid down for truthful speech by Vyasa, and is the very basis of healthy ethical conduct. Yudhishthira's statement in the Mahabharata war: *'Ashwatthama, a man or an elephant has been killed,'* may apparently be a truthful one, but since it was spoken to deceive Dronacharya, it falls under the category of falsehood. Similarly if one makes a true remark in a language unintelligible to the listener, it would not carry any meaning and would not be considered true.

**Truth and Human Welfare**

The third and the most important condition for truthfulness is that it must not be harmful to any one. It is even said that truth is not speaking according to facts; nor is speaking contrary to facts falsehood; but that which conduces to maximum good of creatures must be considered truth. Why? Because the highest truth is that all creatures are one—that there is a solidarity of existence.

One great difficulty with truth is that it is often bitter. Stark realities like disease, old age, and death, are bitter. Injustice, exploitation, and brutal disparities prevalent in the world are bitter truths. Every human being has weaknesses, faults, and defects in character, and conduct which too are unpleasant. The person who tries to observe truth not only has to bear a lot of hardships, but often hurts others too. Observing a vow, keeping one's commitments and promises, entails a lot of struggle, internal and external. Therefore observance of truth as a personal discipline may be laudable, but it must be tempered with modesty and mercy if it conflicts with the interests of others or goes against the greatest good of the greatest number. Modesty, or *sheela*, is an equally noble value which is concerned with the feelings of and the well-being of others. Let us try to understand this with the help of an illustration.

Kaikeyi asked two boons from King Dasharatha. The poor king was trapped. He had promised the boons and could not retract his words. Although he knew that he had been cheated, he could not break his promise, and while holding on to truth — personal truth — he renounced Rama, and also his life.

Was the action of Dasharatha justified? While the king's supreme sacrifice is laudable from the standpoint of personal dharma — the personal observance of truth — it cannot be justified from a social stand point. In succumbing to the intrigues of Manthara and Kaikeyi, King Dasharatha was perpetrating injustice which could have far-reaching consequences, not only for the race of Raghus, but for the society at large.

Contrary to Dasharatha's, and even Rama's conduct, Bharata refused to obey the injunction of the second boon granted by the king to his mother, Kaikeyi. He saw through the foul play and decided to undo the harm already done by bringing back Rama who had already left for the forest in compliance with the first boon. But could he bring back Rama? No. Rama was not willing to return. His argument was that if he were to return at the entreaties of Bharata, the future generations would turn back from an austere and noble path on some pretext or the other. Bharata too realized that there was greater good of the greater number if Rama remained in the forest and did not return before the expiry of the period of exile.

Thus the concept of modesty, or *sheela*, must temper truth and justice, and social good must prevail over personal observance of truth. Otherwise such an observance of truth may turn out to be a vice instead of a virtue.

Every rule has exceptions and this is true of the practice of truth, too. Fables and stories are often used to convey certain values, especially to children. Eulogies and exaggerated statements in the epic stories and mythologies amount to the use of untruth to explain higher, eternal, moral values. *Mahabharata* describes Sri Krishna as making a large number of statements and performing many actions which do not strictly fall under the category of truth, but which were aimed at the greater good.

**Practice of Mental Truth**

As has been pointed out, a practitioner of truth must be extremely careful in his speech and conduct. Such observances naturally make him extremely alert. His whole life becomes an intense and continuous tapas, an austerity. He has to use his will-power at every step. Thus a sincere practice of truthfulness takes an aspirant into a new realm — a mental world as it were.

Practicing truthfulness initially causes a certain amount of inner tension due to a conflict between the higher ideal and the unconquered and suppressed desires and passions. Such inner conflicts find expression sometimes as forgetfulness, "slips of the tongue," unusual dreams, etc. The aspirant may even risk becoming a hypocrite. Swami Vivekananda has said that a large number of people who take to religion become hypocrites.

Society compels us to hide our defects and exhibit only the brighter side of our character. We are not able to make speech and thought one. The practice of truth is essentially the sadhana of making thought, word, and deed correspond.

Sri Ramakrishna never cared for the opinion of others nor tried to act as a "cultured gentleman" to please others. When Maharshi Devendranath Tagore invited him to the prayer meeting of the Brahmo Samaj, he frankly said that although he was willing to attend it, it would not be possible for him to act or dress as a "gentleman."

Sri Ramakrishna's perfect harmony of thought, word, and deed is amazing. He was established in perfect chastity. To test his self-control he allowed Sri Sarada Devi, his wife, to live with him in the same room for months.

Seeing the Holy Mother asleep by his side one night, the Master addressed his own mind and started discriminating,

> "Practicing truthfulness initially causes a certain amount of inner tension due to a conflict between the higher ideal and the unconquered and suppressed desires and passions. Such inner conflicts find expression sometimes as forgetfulness, "slips of the tongue," unusual dreams, etc. The aspirant may even risk becoming a hypocrite. Swami Vivekananda has said that a large number of people who take to religion become hypocrites."

"This is, O mind, a female body. People look upon it as an object of great enjoyment, a thing highly prized, and they die for enjoying it. But if one goes for it, one has to remain obsessed with body consciousness. One cannot go beyond it and realize God, who is Existence-Knowledge-Bliss. Do not, O mind, harbour one thought within and a contrary attitude without. Say in truth whether you want to have it, or God. If you want it, it is here before you; have it." He discriminated thus; but scarcely had he entertained in his mind the idea of touching the person of the Holy Mother, when his mind shrank and at once lost itself so deeply in Samadhi that it did not regain normal consciousness that night.

The significant element in this episode is the fact that Sri Ramakrishna addressed his mind and asked it to act according to its wish so that there may not be the slightest dichotomy between thought and deed, conduct and character. What we intend to stress is that a harmony between thought, word, and deed is the most important aspect of the practice of truthfulness, without which none can get established in truth.

**The Yogic Technique of Truthfulness**

Various means have been suggested for resolving the conflict between thought, word, and deed. The behavioristic school of Western psychology emphasizes behavior or conduct and recommends moulding thoughts according to it. Sigmond Freud has advocated that our desires and passions must be freely expressed. They are natural; to consider them evil and to suppress them causes conflicts and complexes. Hence, according to Freud, if we don't suppress them and act according to them, there won't be conflicts. Others suggest that we must become impartial witnesses of our desires, passions, and conflicts, so that we may transcend them.

> "A practitioner of truth must carefully avoid reading fiction and imaginative literature, and must devote as much time as possible to reading spiritual literature which will help the mind to be in tune with Absolute Reality."

The Indian Yogic technique is, however, different. In this, the mind is trained to contemplate the Absolute Truth, *pàramàrthika satya*. The first step is to totally give up day-dreaming, brooding over the past, or planning for the future. A practitioner of truth must carefully avoid reading fiction and imaginative literature, and must devote as much time as possible to reading spiritual literature which will help the mind to be in tune with Absolute Reality. The life and character of such great heroes like Rama, Harishchandra, and Yudhishthira, who observed truth, must be read and meditated upon.

Patanjali has recommended the technique of raising contrary thoughts when ideas inimical to moral values hinder their practice. When one experiences feelings of hatred, etc., and is tortured by the agonizing fiery passions which lead to wrong courses of conduct, such as "I shall kill him who hurts me, I shall speak untruth, I shall take things belonging to others," he should encourage contrary thoughts. He should contemplate: "*Roasted on the pitiless burning coals of the cycle of births, I took refuge in the virtues of Yoga by promising security to all living beings. After having abjured such perverse thoughts I am behaving like a dog in betaking myself to them. As a dog licks his vomit, so it is for me to take up thoughts and lines of action discarded by me as evil.*"

**Establishment in Truthfulness**

According to the *Mundaka Upanisad*, Truth alone triumphs — *satyameva jayate*. Shankaracharya clarifies this statement by saying that the person who observes truth, triumphs. Apparently and initially, people resorting to falsehood may succeed, but history proves the fact that, ultimately, righteous and truthful people become victorious, and these others fall.

According to Patanjali, "*When truthfulness is achieved, the words (of the yogi) acquire the power of making his intentions fruitful.*" This actually means that whatsoever such a yogi might speak comes to pass. If he says to a person, 'May you be righteous,' the person would indeed become righteous. He who practices truthfulness in thought, word, and deed, for a minimum of twelve years, whose thoughts and words are always strictly in accordance with truth, and who would not speak an untruth even to save his life — such a person develops a tremendous will. His simple, truthful words hold irresistible power, and produce great effects upon listeners — who are compelled to heed and act accordingly.

It is sometimes asked: Suppose a yogi established in truthfulness were to say "May the sun rise in the West," or "Let water turn into stone," will such utterances come true? No. Such a yogi, who has endeavored throughout to avoid all falsehood and act and speak strictly according to truth, would never utter such words against the laws of nature.

It is also said, and confirmed too, that even "slips of the tongue," and words spoken carelessly in unguarded moments by such sages, come true. Here, also, there is a fallacy. How can there be a slip of the tongue or an unguarded or careless moment in a person who has for decades been extremely careful in his words and deeds? Such utterances might appear casual and unguarded, but they are in reality expressions of his insight into the future events obtained by holding to truth. His words reflect God's will, and simply anticipate what will happen. Boons and curses by such sages do not go against the law of karma; they only corroborate it.

What has been described above as the result of the establishment in truthfulness must be considered as a by-product of the observance of truth, and not its ultimate end. For, truth is the aim in itself. It is the goal, as well as the means. This is why Sri Ramakrishna could offer everything to the Divine Mother — dharma and adharma, virtue and vice, action and inaction — but not truth. Indeed, truth is the highest value, the very basis of all values, and the ultimate value of values.

*(This article has been reprinted with the permission of Vedanta Keshari)*

A former editor of the Vedanta Keshari, and previously of the Ramakrishna Mission Home of Service, Swami Brameshananda is a senior monk of the Ramakrishna Order and until recently was the Secretary of the Ramakrishna Mission Ashram in Chandigarh, India. Over the years his writings in Hindi and English have appeared in several journals, including Prabuddha Bharata, Vedanta Keshari, and Nectar of Nondual Truth. He specializes in themes related to Jainism. He is now retired and is living in Varanasi.

# Wisdom Facets From the Gem of Truth

Sri Ramakrishna

Holy Mother, Sri Sarada Devi

### "The Keys of Kundalini"
"An incarnation of God or one born with some of the characteristics of the Incarnation is called an Ishvarakoti. An ordinary man is called a jiva, or a jivakoti. By dint of sadhana a jivakoti can realize God; but after samadhi he cannot come back to the plane of relative consciousness. The Ishvarakoti is like the king's son. He has the keys to all the rooms of the seven-story palace. The jivakoti is like a petty official; he can enter some of the rooms of the palace, but that is his limit."
*(Gospel of Sri Ramakrishna)*

### Meditating Upon God with Form, and Beyond Form
"While wandering in the forest Ramachandra saw a number of rishis. They welcomed Him to their ashrama with great love and said to Him: 'Oh Rama, today our lives are blessed because we have seen You. But we know You as the son of Dasarahtha. Bharadvaja and other sages call you a Divine Incarnation; but that is not our view. We meditate upon the Indivisible Satchidananda.' Rama was pleased and smiled."
*(The Gospel of Sri Ramakrishna)*

### The Worthless Stuff of Worldliness
"Worldly people are in a state of chronic intoxication — mad with lust and gold. They are insensible to spiritual ideas. That is why I love the youngsters. They are good receptacles and may become useful in God's work. But as for worldly people, you lose almost everything while trying to eliminate the worthless stuff in them. They are like bony fish — almost all bones and very little meat."
*(Gospel of Sri Ramakrishna)*

### A Nutritionless Meal for Mother Kali
"I once experienced Divine Mother as a young woman nine months pregnant. She gave birth to the world, cradled it, caressed it, nursed it at her breast, then began to swallow it. As the universe entered Her dark Mouth, it was immediately revealed to me to be void of any substantial or independent existence."
*(Great Swan: Meetings With Ramakrishna)*

### Separating the Wheat from the Chaff
"There is the husk, and there is the grain; public criticism is like the husk. For example, how extensively was Naren censured by the people for going to the West. People soil their clothes, and the washerman cleans them. Those who discuss the misdeeds of others become a party to their sinful acts. Do not speak out unpleasant truths at any time."
*(The Compassionate Mother)*

### Gifts from God, Burdens from Mankind
"Never ask for anything from anyone. Do human gifts last long? But when the Master gives, you will find no place to keep them. The Master's gifts never get exhausted. He that begs gets nothing, and he that begs not gets everything. You should never ask anything from anyone.'"
*(The Compassionate Mother)*

### Heeding the Mind's Original Intentions
"My child, always pay heed to the first suggestion coming from the mind; it usually proves to be right. The other day my health became slightly indisposed. I decided not to take a bath. Later, the mind changed and suggested to me that I go ahead and take a bath because it was a holy day. I took a bath and caught a fever."
*(The Compassionate Mother)*

### "Somewhere Far"
"I was once meditating on Balaram Babu's terrace. I gradually became absorbed in samadhi. Afterwards I remembered that I had gone somewhere far. There, everyone was receiving me and attending on me. I had become, as if, exquisite to look at. The Master was there. I was cordially made to sit near him. And what a bliss it was! I can't describe it in words. When I finally gained awareness of the external world, I found my body lying there. I mused, how, after all, to enter into that despicable thing. I was not at all willing to occupy it again....."
*(The Compassionate Mother)*

# Wisdom Facets From the Gem of Truth

Swami Vivekananda        Disciples & Devotees of Sri Ramakrishna

### In the Jungle, the Lion Sleeps — then Awakens

"Within there is a lion — the eternally pure, illumined, and ever-free Atman. And directly one realizes Him through meditation and concentration, the world of Maya vanishes. He is equally present in all; and the more one practices, the quicker does the Kundalini awaken in him. When that power reaches the head, one's vision becomes unobstructed, and one realizes the Atman." *(Talks with Swami Vivekananda)*

### When You are Ready, take Sattvic Food Only

"All liking for fish and meat disappears when pure sattva is highly developed. The signs of its manifestation in a soul are sacrifice of everything for others, perfect nonattachment to lust and wealth, and want of pride and egoism. The want of animal food goes away when these things are seen in a man." *(Talks With Swami Vivekananda)*

### Knowing "That," All Else is Known

"Know Him, think of Him, by which knowing all else is known. And when that Atman is realized, the purport of all the scriptures will be perceived as easily as a fruit in the palm of your hand. Try to manifest that Atman, and you will see your intellect penetrating into all subjects. The intellect of one who has not realized the Atman is one-sided, whereas the genius of the knower of Atman is all-embracing." *(Talks With Swami Vivekananda)*

### My Life as the Atman

"In this embodied existence you will be tossed again and again on the waves of happiness and misery, prosperity and adversity — but know them all to be of momentary duration. Never care for them. 'I am the birthless, the deathless Atman, whose nature is intelligence' — implanting this idea firmly in your heart, you should pass the days of your life." *(Talks with Swami Vivekananda)*

### Pray for His Inspired Mood!

"Sometimes I feel like entreating and imploring students to go on with their spiritual practices. At other times I see that the Lord is everything: the Lord is the cause, the Lord is the doer, the Lord is the instrument, and the Lord is the deed. He is all and everywhere. I see Him playing in so many forms. Then who am I to give instructions to? Why should people accept my words? However, when the inspiration comes from the Lord, people do accept my words, and follow them." *(Swami Brahmananda, The Eternal Companion)*

### The Acid Test for Personal Advancement

"Compassion and blessings are undoubtedly upon the followers of Sri Ramakrishna and Swamiji. But can deep-rooted samskaras be replaced in a day? They are erased gradually. Make up your minds now and plunge into sadhana. Then only will you see for yourselves whether you are making progress or not. One must labor hard to realize the Truth." *(Swami Saradananda, in Glimpses of a Great Soul)*

### The Witness of Ordinary Mind

"Troubles arise when there is slackness in spiritual practices. So, one has to do the Lord's work without any attachment. A fall comes as soon as egoism and attachment come. The Master used to say that there should be no self-deception in the matter of sticking to the Ideal. Therefore, one should keep strict vigilance over the mind, analyzing it at every turn." *(Swami Sivananda, For Seekers of God)*

### Why Not Just Forget Mind & Prana?

"Scientific evidence can be given in support of the argument that mind is not the same as the brain. Their relationship is intimate, so most beings cannot separate them. So the mind as an entity is not considered as a reality. They also deny the existence of the vital force as distinct from other forces of nature. To them, the causes of diseases are only physical." *(Swami Abhedananda, Psychic Phenomena)*

# SCRIPTURAL SAYINGS
## of the World's Religious Traditions

"We are astonished to see that there have been and still are men who kill their kind in order to eat them. But the time will come when our grandchildren will be astonished that their grandparents killed every day millions of animals in order to eat them when one can have a sound and substantial nourishment by the use of the fruits of the earth."

"That nameless, formless Brahman, out of Which sprang the Holy Trinity at the beginning of a cosmic cycle, and Who delivered the Vedas unto Lord Brahma; who is partless, faultless, actionless, and Divine. Who resembles fire that has consumed all its fuel. I go for refuge in that Supreme Brahman, Whose Light turns the attention of mankind towards the Atman – the indivisible Self in all beings, all things."

"If a man say, 'I love God,' but hateth his brother, he is a liar. For he that loveth not his brother whom he has seen, how then can he love God who he hath not seen? And so I say, little children, let us not love in word, neither in tongue, but in deed and in truth. And hereby we know that we are of the truth."

"So what of your trials. Others had trials of mockings and scourging, yea, moreover of bonds and imprisonment. Many were stoned, while others were sawn asunder, were tortured, were slain with the sword. They wandered about in sheepskins and goatskins, being destitute, afflicted, tormented, of whom the world was not worthy. They wandered about in deserts and over mountains, and slept in slave-dens and caves in the earth."

"The world is a brilliant flame in which every moment a new creature burns itself. Bravely turn thine eyes from it like the lion, if thou would'st not burn thyself in it like the butterfly. The insensate one who, like that insect, adores the flame, will surely come to be consumed in it. So find a good and true guide and swiftly and wisely issue forth out of the pit of the world."

"The superior being always remains aware of the middle path, and perseveres in its practice. Even if he remains unknown, and the world esteems him not, he feels no regret on that account. It is only the illumined sage who is capable of maintaining such a sublime state."

BHAVATARINI MA/JOCELYNE NIELSEN, R.N.

# The Role of Peace in Healing

TRUE PEACE can be defined as freedom from mental and spiritual disturbances such as conflict arising from passion, desires, attachment, sense of guilt, etc. This freedom brings quiet, calm, tranquility, and will lead one to equanimity, balance, and well being.

The process to attain peace requires that one become conscious, aware of Awareness. At the mental/emotional level one of the processes to attain peace is to identify the source of stress, pain, worry, anxiety, fear and then release or let go of the resistance. This resistance exists in the unconscious programming generated from karma — the accumulated effect of past action stored in the subconscious mind. To release and let go at the mental and emotional level requires forgiveness, apologies, the blessings of all the parties involved, including oneself, and neutralization of all situations and conditions which were the cause of the initial distress in the first place. By practicing this method, harmony and freedom in the emotional body can be achieved, leading to the descent of overall quiescence.

Webster's Dictionary defines healing as *"the action of restoration of wholeness, well being, safety, and prosperity."* Thus, it is the process of curing a diseased condition and recovering from sickness. Further, to heal is *"to purify, to cleanse, to repair, to restore from sin, grief, despair, danger, and distraction."* Healing also strives to make the body whole or sound so that its functions are duly and efficiently discharged. Thus, real health is a state of homeostasis wherein all the levels of consciousness are in harmony. Being healed also means being at peace.

The power of healing functions, then, on holistic, religious and spiritual levels of human awareness as well. Holistic healing is conceived of as a thorough restoration and alignment of body, mind, and spirit. Due to individual, familial, and societal karma, beings develop illnesses and imbalances in body, mind, and spirit. Working these out is necessary for wholeness and holiness both. There cannot be health, outer peace, without inner peace. Yet, it is also important to note that in life, in relativity, there will always be illness and disharmony at some level of consciousness. Ironically, some of the best learned lessons come when a being is experiencing ill health.

At the spiritual level, supplication or prayer, and meditation have been employed throughout the history of the human race as the best way to attain and retain peace and equanimity. "Peace be with you" is repeated in all religions on a daily basis, and confers an effect of calmness and healing on everyone. Therefore, it is easy to see that the attainment of peace brings about healing. True healing thus requires inner peace. The road for the attainment of inner peace has many approaches. Some beings are born with or develop physical illnesses. They spend most of their lives learning to find inner peace while dealing with the pain and suffering of the body. It is said that the last manifestation of an illness or imbalance is in the physical body. It is easier to address and find a cure in the body than in the mind. If the mind stuff (chitta) is not dealt with, the illness will return. For instance, in Chinese Medicine, a liver disease is associated with anger, resentment, depression, control, lack of trust. The liver is the organ of purification. To heal the liver requires that the thoughts and behaviors associated with the organ be changed. To attain inner peace and heal the liver demands total surrender to the Higher Self and the absolute trust that follows.

We have memories and remnants of the healing arts and customs of earlier Eastern civilizations. Chinese, Tibetan, and Ayurvedic medicines still employ treatments which address body, mind, and spirit. These healing systems, founded on a spiritual basis, rest in the hands of spiritually developed practitioners who can guide the sick in understanding the cause of their illnesses and find the proper cure.

The present age has made it difficult to create healing envi-

Bhavatarini Ma, Jocelyne Nielsen, R.N., M.S., C.N.S., now retired, was the founder and director of the Healing Center of San Francisco, and resident head of the Sarada, Ramakrishna, Vivekananda Association (SRV) of San Francisco. She served many decades as a clinical nurse specialist in psychiatric/mental health nursing, and as a holistic practitioner.

ronments for sick people. In ancient Greece there were Aesclepius temples where sick people went to be healed. Healers would pray over patients as well as administer medicines and herbal concoctions. Massages, healing water baths, and personal counseling helped repair body, mind, and emotions. Some beings are born with or develop mental illnesses. They also need to surrender and require a great deal of assistance and personal discipline to quiet the distortion of the mind. Others are born with spiritual restlessness. They need to seek spiritual guidance and hopefully encounter the appropriate practices such as self-control, discrimination, detachment, and an enlightened spiritual teacher who will guide them towards true healing — Self-realization.

Using the Adhara system of Vedanta, we can measure health and peace to see if the sheaths covering the Atman are in disharmony. Is the annamaya kosha, the food body, receiving adequate nutrients, proper rest, exercise, adequate hydration, regular cleanliness? In the pranamaya kosha, the energy body, are the five pranas flowing correctly through the subtle breath of the body? Has the manomaya kosha, the mental body, purged itself of false premises and habitual patterns of thinking? Has the vijnanamaya kosha, the intellect, risen beyond limited knowledge and dwarfed understanding? Has the anandamaya kosha, the bliss state, reestablished its connection with the Divine and transcended mundane pleasure-seeking?

To conclude, peace of mind requires self-love and self-acceptance which brings about peace of heart. Peace of heart and peace of mind are crucial prerequisites for comprehensive healing. Jesus of Nazareth cured people and freed them from maladies and infirmities by transmitting peace to their soul. Ramakrishna touched his disciples and gave them peace and experiences of enlightenment. May we, by the Grace of God, the Guru, and our own self-effort be granted peace and healing that surpasses all understanding.

ALEXANDER HIXON

# AN INTERVIEW WITH MOTHER TERESA

*Sometime in the mid 1970's, our SRV founder, Lex Hixon, was able to schedule an interview with Mother Teresa at her Bronx, New York, Mission Home. This interview took place just after her address to the United Nations — an inspiring talk that caught the deep attention of all present that day.*

## Address

I am grateful to God to be able to be with you today. Because I stand here for our people, our brothers and sisters, who have been created by the same, loving hand of God — one God; the God of Love. And He has created us in His own image.

Therefore, we have been created to love. Faith in action is love, and love in action is service. God loved the world so much that He gave His own son, Jesus Christ, to us, to be amongst us, to be one of us, to be like us in all things — except sin — that we may be able through this human body to come as close as possible to the Divine and love him as he has loved us. Christ lived a few years of a human life with us, going about doing good, and continually stressing that one point; that we are one, that we are His, that we belong to his Father; that His Father has made us for Himself. He continually kept on saying, *"Love one another as I have loved you. As the Father has loved me, I have loved you."* And we know how He loved us, dying on the cross. And from beneath the cross, you and I stand and look at each other. And we wonder, do we really love as he has loved us?

Thousands and thousands of people today are hungry, and naked, and homeless. They are our brothers and sisters. They belong to the same family, to the same loving God. To make us realize, Christ has said — and Christ cannot deceive: *"I was hungry, and you gave me something to eat. And I was sick, and in prison, and you visited me. I was naked, and you clothed me. I was homeless, and you took me in."* He made himself the poorest of the poor so that, at the hour of death, he might be able to tell us — to tell you, to tell me, *"Come, all ye blessed of my Father: because, when I was hungry you gave me food to eat; not only bread, but I was hungry for love, to be wanted, to be known, to be somebody to somebody. I was naked and you clothed me; not only with a piece of cloth, but with that human dignity. I was homeless, and you took me in; not only in that little room made of stones, but in your heart, and covered me with that understanding love. You took me as your brother, your sister; you leadeth to me."* How wonderful is the greatness of Christ's love, for each one of us.

Let us today — when we have gathered to prove to the whole world that we are one — let us be one in this love to the poorest of the poor in the world, that we recognize him in them, that they are our brothers and sisters. Do we know where they are? Do we know what it is to be hungry? Do we know what it is to be lonely? To be unwanted? To be uncared for? To be helpless? To have forgotten what it is to smile? To have forgotten what is that human touch? Do we know? Do we know our poor here in the United States? Do we know our poor in our own home — the lonely ones, the unwanted ones? Do we know that the unborn child is the unwanted one; that I, the poorest of the poor, do not want that child? How terrible it is to think that our little brothers and sisters, created by the same loving hand of God, are unwanted, unloved. This is the greatest poverty.

Let us today pray together that you and I bring peace into the world, and not by just doing small things and forgetting. Our poor people don't need our pity; they need our love, our compassion, for they are very great people, very lovable people. We don't know them; that's why we can't love them. And because we cannot love them, we do not serve them.

And that's why Jesus, again and again and again, has repeated himself: *"Love one another as I have loved you."* He has loved us until it hurt him. Do we love? Do we really want to love until it hurts? By our love, by the recognizing of our brothers and sisters that live in the gutters — and with them, like one of them whom I picked up who said, "I have lived like an animal in the streets; but I am going to die like an angel, loved and cared for."

Just a few weeks ago, I picked up a woman from the streets, from the open drain, and brought her to the "Home For The Dying." And I knew that she was dying. And after I did whatever I could do for her, she took hold of my hand. There was a very beautiful smile on her face as she said one word only; "Thank you." She gave me more than I gave her. Her love for me was greater than mine for her. Thank you.

## Interview

**Mother Teresa:** There is a very beautiful prayer of Cardinal Newman, and also St. Francis of Assisi, that states, *"Make me an instrument of Thy Peace."* Yesterday I wanted to mention it in my address, but it slipped my mind completely [laughs]. It is just beautiful.

**Lex Hixon:** The talk was very good, though. I think everyone felt moved by it.

**Mother Teresa:** It was the Truth, I know; we can't make up these things. These aren't the people, this is the Truth of Christ. Like in that beautiful prayer by Cardinal Newman, *"Jesus: help me to spread thy fragrance everywhere I go. Guard my soul with your Spirit and Life. Penetrate and possess my whole being so utterly that all my life may only be a radiance of yours. Shine through me and be showing me that every soul I come in contact with may feel your presence in my soul. Let them look up and see only Jesus. Stay with me, and then I shall begin to shine as you shine, so to shine as to be a light to others. The light of Jesus will be all from thee; none of it will be*

> "And it is very beautiful that we get so many young people who are joining, giving their lives totally to God, to bring hope, and light, and joy into the lives of so many who want love. And they know exactly what they want; they want a challenge, the young people today. They want the life of poverty, the life of prayer, and of sacrifice. This will lead them to the service of the poor, which is very beautiful; and very dignified, knowingly to chose like that. And it is not the work only, work is only a means. To find what they want, that is only Jesus."

*mine. It will be you shining on others through me. Let me thus praise thee in the way you love best, by shining on those around me. Let me preach thee without preaching — not by words, but by my example. By the catching force, the sympathetic influence of what we do, the evident fullness of the Love, my heart begs for Thee. Amen."*

**Lex Hixon:** Great. Very lovely.

**Mother Teresa:** It's because I think his coming is coming up. So I say, we will leave this prayer to the full Light, then, and there will be only Jesus. I will never be able to see anything; only Jesus. So we only live that life of prayer and sacrificing. [microphone falls down]

**Lex Hixon,** (laughing)**:** Even the microphone is hiding away.

**Mother Teresa:** People are more and more hungry for God; you can see that everywhere. There, the poor have no difficulty, because there is nothing to suffer. For the richer ones it is more difficult. For the rich, suffering gets to them, and it becomes an obstacle. Even Jesus said that. But people are beginning to get more and more awakened to the presence of the poor and their welfare, getting more and more concerned, and having more desires for sharing, and bringing new hope and new life into the lives of those who have lost hope.

And I think that we all are of the same family, and come from the same loving hand; its penetrating more and more in the world. And for us who know Jesus, and know what he has said, and that he will not deceive us, and that he said he will *"leadeth to me,"* we spend twenty-four hours touching him. For me, knowingly, and for the others, perhaps, unknowingly, we are always touching the body of Christ. Because, at the hour of death we are all going to be judged, Christian and non-Christian, for what we have done for the naked, the poor, the homeless. And that is for all of us. Does not matter who you are or what you are. We need to realize that more and more, and that is when a better understanding is coming to the people. And I think that it is works of love that will produce peace in the world.

And it is very beautiful that we get so many young people who are joining, giving their lives totally to God, to bring hope, and light, and joy into the lives of so many who want love. And they know exactly what they want; they want a challenge, the young people today. They want the life of poverty, the life of prayer, and of sacrifice. This will lead them to the service of the poor, which is very beautiful; and very dignified, knowingly to choose like that. And it is not the work only, work is only a means. To find what they want, that is only Jesus.

It is very hard to find Jesus; you need to be completely free, to be able to love him with undivided love and chastity, and be free through poverty. It is very difficult. Unless there is that freedom you cannot have that. *"Blessed are the pure of heart, for they shall see God."* That is where cleanliness of heart comes in, freedom through poverty. Only, our poor people are forced to be poor. The choice to be poor is very beautiful.

**Lex Hixon:** What is poverty of Spirit? What is meant by that term?

**Mother Teresa:** In that spiritual poverty, there is the emptiness you feel that you are nothing. That is poverty of Spirit, right? But there is spiritual poverty, knowing God. In this Western world, there is much more of that, much more of that then the material poverty that we face in Africa and India. It is easier to satisfy. There is a hungry woman. I give her a plate of rice, and it is finished, all satisfied. But people like here, and in Rome, and London, a plate of rice is not going to satisfy. They don't need that. That terrible loneliness, that helplessness, that unwantedness — that complete darkness of the self — that is great poverty.

So what is holiness? It is to allow Christ to live his life in us. Passion, joy, success — that is the gift of God. So suffering is a means to share in the redemption of the world.

**Lex Hixon:** Do you feel greatly saddened by suffering, or do you feel that you are untouched by it to some extent?

**Mother Teresa:** Ummm, not really untouched. For example, there were the refugees, and we then had this terrible famine and things like that; you feel that the passion of Christ is greatly relived once more. And then you try to share in your own faith. And when you see the people suffering so much, like here in this area — so much suffering, so much loneliness, so much pain, so much of hurt. It is like Calvary, though in a different form. It is Christ's pain, going through his agony again. That's so difficult to believe.

**Lex Hixon:** My wife and I were very moved by Padre Pio. We have read of him.

**Mother Teresa:** Yes.

**Lex Hixon:** He felt the pain all his life; he did not try to transcend it. He didn't leave it behind.

**Mother Teresa:** No. He shared it. That was his way of sharing in the passion of Christ. And you, each one of us, if we really keep close to Jesus, then the nails and the crown have to hurt us a little bit. The closer you get, then the greater is the hurt. That is natural. *"I and my Father are One. I have to do the will of my Father."* Christ again and again has insisted on that. The whole time, we have to make God the center of our prayer, of our life, of our everything. Without that there is no question of our coming together, or understanding each other, or accepting one another. We cannot choose something outside; we have to choose something from within. And that within must be One.

**Lex Hixon:** As well as your very active life, do you have times where you take retreats and just pray?

**Mother Teresa:** Yes. We have eight days retreat, then three days, and every week we have one day of recollection. And we spend four hours a day praying. Then every day, one hour of adoration after we finish the work, and maybe two hours in the morning for prayer and meditation. So we use the solace of the poor to put our love for God into action. We put all of our prayers into action, but action is only a means to an end. Our lives are very much woven into the Eucharist, for if we can't see Christ in the appearance of bread, it would be difficult for us to see Him in the appearance of the poor. That is why we need our lives completely woven into the Eucharist; it then becomes very simple. Then we are content living in the One, for we are touching his body twenty-four hours.

And that is the beautiful part, and he will not deceive us. Without that we wouldn't be able to stand it. We wouldn't be able to continue with the work. Every day we have this continual oneness with Christ. He explains this very beautifully with the vine and the branches, and the Father the Gardener and the fruit, and all that. Just exactly like that, it is what our life needs to be; just a branch. But he does everything [Mother Teresa laughs]. So I wanted to say yes.

**Lex Hixon:** Can you give us an example of the prayers and meditation that you do? Are there any prayers that you do that you say to yourself inwardly that we could hear? Would you be willing to share anything like that with us?

**Mother Teresa:** Ahhhh! [silence] That's very difficult. But I think everything is in Christ, no? That he is God from God, Light from Light. He is equal to God in all things. He is the deep substance of the heart, and he has chosen us for his own. That recitation that he is God from God, Light from Light, Truth from Truth, I believe.

**Lex Hixon:** Do you visualize the radiant Christ as you repeat those words?

**Mother Teresa:** No. He's there. [soft laughter] That's why it is difficult to speak of prayer. Because all of us have a different way of touching God, and being touched by God — each one. Some people find it easy to speak about it, some people find it difficult. And so he is glorified in both ways. [more laughter] But we have the Gospel, and the scriptures are always there. And quite often by repeating them, like the 15th chapter of St. John, and repeating it again, it is the most beautiful prayer.

**Lex Hixon:** Would you be willing to read from the 15th chapter of St. John?

**Mother Teresa:** I don't have my glasses with me.

**Lex Hixon:** Will you get her glasses for her? [shuffling]

**Mother Teresa, reading:** "I am the vine; I am the true vine, and my Father is the vine dresser. Every branch in me that bears no fruit, He cuts away, and every branch that does bear fruit He prunes, to make it bear even more. You are pruned already, by reason of the word that I have spoken to you. Make your home in Me, as I make mine in you. As a branch cannot bear fruit unless remain part of the vine, neither can you, unless you remain in Me. I am the vine, you are the branches. Whoever remains in Me, with Me in him, there is fruit in plenty. For without Me you can do nothing. Anyone who does not remain in Me is like a branch that has been thrown away. Even thus, these branches are collected and thrown on the fire, and they are burned. If you remain in Me, and My words remain in you, you may ask what you will and you shall get it."

**Lex Hixon:** Very Lovely!

**Mother Teresa:** This is the place where he said, "Love one another." [continuing to read scripture] "It is through the glory of my Father that you shall bear much fruit, and then you will be my disciples. As the Father has loved me, so, I have loved you. Then remain with my love. If you keep my commandments you will remain in my love, just as I have kept my Father's commandments and I remain in His love. I have told you this so that my own joy will be in you, and your joy will be complete. This is my commandment. Love one another as I have loved you." [bell rings for prayer]

**Lex Hixon:** We wouldn't want to keep you any longer. Thank you very much!

[For this and over 350 other SRV interviews, visit srv.org]

> "Our lives are very much woven into the Eucharist, for if we can't see Christ in the appearance of bread, it would be difficult for us to see Him in the appearance of the poor. That is why we need our lives completely woven into the Eucharist; it then becomes very simple. Then we are content living in the One, for we are touching his body twenty-four hours."

◆ ANNAPURNA SARADA

# RESURRECTION OF THE DHARMIC FAMILY
## Awakening and Nurturing Inner Spirituality

*In today's world, mention is made of the importance of raising children, that they are our most important "resource," — our future. The word in itself suggests a "re"turn to our "source," and if that becomes for us a real crying need and a sincere desire, all of the nations, cultures, societies, and peoples of the world would have to sit down together in earnest and seriously "re"define the word. If we believe and cling to the idea that our chief resource be material in nature — what is transitory, ever-changing and decaying — rather than spiritual in nature — that which is abiding, stable, and eternal — then we sell short not only ourselves, our lives and our unlimited potential, but the lives and futures of our children and generations to come as well.*

For many decades now in our society we have witnessed a downward spiral into preoccupation with material well-being. The acquisition of wealth by honest means and the satisfaction of legitimate desires are not negative occupations. However, *preoccupation* with them, which means taking them to be the purpose of life, and seeking them at the expense of the well-being of others and the environment, distorts the character of human beings and creates a malaise throughout society. Seeking pleasure and entertainment then becomes the goal of each individual. People marry out of the desire for pleasure; people hope their jobs will net them enough money in order to buy pleasure; children are brought into the world for the pleasure and/or security of the parents. And then many children are raised with the mantra, "go have fun."

Some of us are aware of the increasingly superficial atmosphere of society in general. Family life, more often than not, fails to create strong characters, deep thinkers, or persons capable of working selflessly for the good of family and society. Even more rare is the family that exposes their children to those truths that will lead them to peace, equanimity, and freedom of the Soul — the greatest gift we can give our children! — and which also conduce to the greatest power for benefitting the world.

### The Superlative Yogic Perspective

According to Yogic psychology, this habitual mode of living life on the surface of existence, seeking enjoyments and avoiding pain, creates a samskara in the mind — a mental impression that accompanies the individual from lifetime to lifetime until a stronger impression is made to counteract it, or it is destroyed in Self-realization. "Seeking enjoyments and avoiding pain" is a shorthand phrase that encompasses all the actions that ordinary people engage in to get what they want and avoid what they do not want, and which causes good, bad, and mixed karmas and samskaras to accumulate. These all necessitate future births to work them out. Understanding and accepting this perspective (which according to both Vedanta and Buddhism represents the first steps toward true freedom) puts the responsibility for our tendencies on our own actions in this life and in prior lifetimes, revealing that we have the power to remake our character and destiny by changing our actions and habits through knowledge and practice. As Lord Vasishtha says in Vasishtha's Yoga: "*Self-effort is of two categories: that of past births and that of this birth. The latter effectively counteracts the former. Fate is none other than self-effort of a past incarnation. There is constant conflict between these two in this incarnation; and that which is more powerful triumphs.*"

It is far too simplistic to excuse our pleasure and security-seeking society on the Great Depression, on the experiences of immigrants fleeing war-torn and famine-stricken societies, on the greed of corporations inflaming our desires with advertising, or the presumed failure of religions — at best, these only perpetuate tendencies that are already present which we ourselves have created. And this is a very significant point. The company that we keep, and that we allow our children to keep, the atmosphere that we choose to live in can either strengthen the positive or the negative tendencies latent within us and our children.

### What the Rishis Bequeathed Us

Ancient, harmonious societies, such as the one that existed during the Vedic period in India, have left records and teachings promoting both the material well-being of people (*Abhyudaya*) and their highest good, based upon transcendence of material nature (*Nihshreyasa*) [see Nectar #12, "The Two Vedic Ideals"]. Swami Vivekananda enshrined this twofold requirement for a dharmic society and individual in the motto of the Ramakrishna Order: "*For the realization of the Self and the good of the world.*" The material well-being of people and society was and is considered of great importance but must be put in the service of the highest good, which is Self-Realization and the freedom, peace, and ultimate fulfillment that accompanies it.

#### *Four Fruits of Life*

Dharma/Divine Life
Artha/Wealth by honest means
Kama/Satisfaction of legitimate desires
Moksha/Liberation

From the Indian philosophy comes a similar or supporting teaching called the Four Fruits of Life. It consists of: Divine life (*dharma*), right livelihood (*artha*), satisfaction of legitimate

> "Our desires and cravings become attenuated as we turn more to what is eternal. We become less selfish. In this way, seeking wealth and satisfaction of earthly desires are easily put in the service of worshiping God in all beings."

desires *(kama)*, and spiritual liberation *(moksha)*. Dharma, a divinely oriented life, heads the list; for without it, the acquisition of wealth and the satisfaction of desires merely increases one's thirst for more and constricts the human spirit into the narrow confines of self-gratification. Seeking and experiencing pleasure from the vast array of objects in our lives will never quench our longing for satisfaction. We are Infinite, and the Infinite can never be fulfilled by the finite. With Divine life at the front, God, the infinite, eternal Essence permeating all beings and objects, including ourselves, is known simultaneously as the highest Ideal of life and the ultimate Source of all fulfillment. Instead of seeking satisfaction from objects, human beings, and situations, that inevitably pass away over time, we come to realize that what satisfaction we do derive is really due to the presence of God permeating those things. Our desires and cravings become attenuated as we turn more to what is eternal. We become less selfish. In this way, seeking wealth and satisfaction of earthly desires are easily put in the service of worshiping God in all beings.

## Defining a Dharmic Life

What are the ingredients of a dharmic life, a divine life? Holy Company is most often the first requirement mentioned. Swami Vivekananda, in his Bhakti Yoga teachings, states that spirituality is ignited and transmitted to us by another person of pure mind and spiritual realization. In his or her company the cravings for ordinary pleasures diminish and love for God grows. Along with holy company, worship of God (one's chosen Ideal of God or the Self) is enjoined, as is study of the revealed scriptures, meditation, and the practice of working without desire for the results.

## Pancha Yajna — The Five Daily Sacrifices

All these aspects of a dharmic life are brought into play in the practice of the Five Daily Sacrifices [see Nectar #7, *Hearing Vedanta — Sacrifice*]. Here, the meaning of "sacrifice" *(yajna)* is defined as reverent worship and selfless service combined. The Five Sacrifices, which is a beautiful melding of social welfare and the highest good, was and is a practice that is to be fully integrated into one's daily life. These five consist of:

*Deva-yajna*, sacrifice to God: Daily worship of God (one's highest conception of the Divine Being) through devotional ritual and the heart's love, chanting the divine Names, devotional singing, meditation on one's Chosen Ideal, and meditation on the stainless Self.

*Rishi-yajna*, sacrifice to the Spiritual Teachers: Daily study of the teachings of the illumined beings, chanting of passages from the scriptures, and reciting stories of their lives and deeds.

*Pitri-yajna*, sacrifice to the ancestors: Our ancestors are an important link for us. It behooves us to know and honor their beneficial contributions, emulate their good qualities, and continue to pass on their knowledge.

*Nara-yajna*, sacrifice to human beings: Worshiping God in human beings by giving food to the hungry, education, health care for the sick — whatever the best and highest service that the person standing before you requires for their material well-being — and supporting centers of spiritual practice whereby people can awaken to their highest good, their true spiritual nature.

### *Five Daily Sacrifices*
Deva Yajna/Sacrifice to God
Rishi Yajna/Sacrifice to the Great Teachers
Pitri Yajna/Sacrifice to the Ancestors
Nara Yajna/Sacrifice to Human Beings
Bhuta Yajna/Sacrifice to Other Beings

*Bhuta-yajna*, sacrifice to other beings: This entire universe, and our own Earth is sentient due to that one Supreme Consciousness pervading everything. Thus, the earth, the environment, the atmospheres, the waters, the minerals, the plants, and animals are all "beings." This sacrifice is a daily, practical, loving stewardship of creatures and environment all based upon this ultimate truth of nonseparation, not just money-making.

To conclude, the essential point in these "sacrifices" is that we are never separate from God, the Great Teachers, the ancestors, other human beings, and other beings due to the all-pervading Divine Being. These Five Daily Sacrifices — which are really universal principles for a divine and harmonious life — performed daily and taught to our children have the power to set in motion a resurgence of dharmic families, dharmic and just societies, and illumined beings.

## No Such Thing as a "Foreign" Religion

Imagine how our communities would be if families began to institute and maintain such regimens. Can we consider putting these teachings into practice in our lives — in our complicated, secularized, and religiously polarized American society? Many may think that the arena of discussion and objection is so vast as to stagger the imagination and discourage one's will to make the attempt. We have so many religions and sects of religions; so many people without a philosophy behind their mode of life; so many struggling just to exist; so many seeking a way out of emptiness and mentally dulled by the internet and surface pastimes. But the point of this article and the urgent need to sow the seeds of a reinvigorated family and society, is not to set things right all at once — as if that could be done. It is simply to begin where we are. To open the door in front of each of us.

The criticism is sometimes raised that taking a "foreign" system and applying it to another culture cannot work. However,

> "The criticism is sometimes raised that taking a 'foreign' system and applying it to another culture cannot work. However, when speaking in terms of spiritual systems for conscious human development and enlightenment, deeper reflection certainly suggests that in essence, none are truly foreign, but rather natural to the aspirations of human beings."

when speaking in terms of spiritual systems for conscious human development and enlightenment, deeper reflection certainly suggests that in essence, none are truly foreign, but rather natural to the aspirations of human beings. Take for instance the Vedic system of the Four Ashramas, the Four Stages of Life.

## The Four Stages of Life

In this system, which is both spiritual and social, a divine life cycle is laid out in tune with material well-being and highest good. In its sweep it naturally incorporated practices already described above in the Five Sacrifices.

### Four Ashramas/Stages of Life

Brahmacharya/Student Stage
Grhastha/Householder Stage
Vanaprastha/Forest-dweller Stage
Sannyasa/Renunciate Stage

*Brahmacharya:* The first stage, student life, consists of acquiring knowledge of the ancient seers and noble ancestors of the past from the adept or illumined teachers of the present, as well as one's parents. As a child, one participates and helps one's parents in the Five Sacrifices. One's childhood is then spent learning the theory and the details of how to live life according to high ideals — moral, ethical, compassionate, and liberating (those teachings and disciplines that go beyond moral and ethical) — for the purpose of realizing and communing with God/Self. Also very important, is that the child is instructed in the responsibilities of each of the four stages of life.

*Grhastha:* When the child becomes an adult and can choose to marry, he or she enters the stage of the householder well-equipped with the knowledge that makes it possible to live life contentedly, without undue suffering, and to serve God in all beings (one's family and all others) in a spirit of selflessness and worship that is founded on a firm understanding of the nature of Reality and the nature of the world. With a spouse, also so instructed, a dharmic family is raised and society is supported by their work and efforts (for it is the householder that creates the wealth of society, thus providing its material well-being, and supports those who move on to the later stages of life). The children of these parents, in their turn, receive spiritual support and instruction from awakened parents and adept teachers, just as their parents had. Please note that the prime ingredient of a divine life, holy company, is present in all these stages.

*Vanaprastha:* When the children are capable of supporting themselves, the parents enter the third stage of life wherein they withdraw from social and family responsibilities and begin to devote themselves more and more to realization of the Ideals they have contemplated and practiced through and alongside their activities at home and in society. Knowledge and experience must culminate in Divine Communion/Self-Realization.

*Sannyasa:* The third stage is a deeper preparation for this, and the fourth stage is a profound renunciation, both inner and outer, which really translates as a complete identification of one's Self with God alone. In most cases it is from these last two stages of life that adept teachers and illumined beings are drawn, who transmit the teachings to the next generation.

## Stopping Short of the True Goal

And here is another essential point: the life of the householder, lived so nobly and generously for the good of all, is not the final stage of life in this system. If we look around ourselves, however, this is not what we see. Rather, people get married, many before learning any skills in the art of divine life, have children, have grandchildren and even great grandchildren, and never move to the next stage. Retirement from familial and social responsibilities usually means trying to enjoy the last years of one's life via pleasurable pastimes, rather than diving deeper into the Sublime, the Ineffable.

Though people may complain of foreign religions and practices, it is really this state of affairs that is "foreign," and not the systems related above. Many societies of the past had stages of instruction, child-bearing and raising, followed by stages of wise elderhood. It is common these days in New Age circles, among the religiously "turned off," and converts to Eastern religions, to put the blame for the lack of depth in our society, for empty dogmas, mindless ritualism, and the narrow and insincere piety experienced in their childhood on the Jewish and Christian religions. But just a little thought and reasoning will reveal that Judaism and Christianity also encompass this natural progression of human unfoldment. The problem is not Religion but how it is interpreted and followed, for all religious paths have as their culmination some form of communion with God which requires one's full attention and devotion. Each religion has its Prophets or Incarnations, saints and sages, married and sometimes monastic, that epitomize the spirit of that religion and model how each stage of life has its own inherent ways in which to practice and prepare for this communion, and which leads one further.

Therefore, let us begin to live a divine life for the benefit of the world, the spiritual health of our children, and for the highest good of all.

---

Annapurna Sarada lives in Honoka'a, Hawai'i, where she serves as the President of SRV Associations and manages SRV publications. She also is the Associate Editor of Nectar of Nondual Truth.

# DISCERNING DIVINE LIFE AND WORLDLY LIFE
## *Renunciation is not Condemnation; It is Deification*

The saints and sages of India, in an effort to help people free themselves from unnecessary suffering, point out the binding influence of worldly life, "mundane human convention," with its surface pastimes and karma-producing attachments. Eshanatrayam, in particular, describes the triple bondage of spouse, wealth, and progeny. At the same time, as seen in the article on page 30, there is the dharmic householder. These people also marry, create wealth, enjoy pleasures, and have children. What is the difference? Basic points are given in the box below.

By way of introduction to these points, it is important to understand that spiritual freedom comes to those who give up thinking that the world and its experiences are the goal of life, and start thinking in terms of the Eternal, the Unchanging. The fully illumined soul, Sri Ramakrishna Paramahamsa, tells us that whether we are monastics or householders, everyone must renounce; monastics renounce outwardly and inwardly, while the householders renounce inwardly. This is, at first, the devout practice of or a firm resolve to remain inwardly content. Eventually, contentment becomes a constant attainment. Pain may be inevitable while occupying the human body, but suffering is different. Suffering is the result of dashed expectations: that the body will always be healthy; that our loved ones will not die; that people will be nice to us; that we will live in comfort always. Does this mean we don't try to improve our situations? Not at all. However, as soon as we desire the results of our actions, then suffering comes if we do not get what we want; and if we do get what we wanted, it just sets us up for remaining in this see-saw of pleasure and pain, attachment and aversion. The world then "calls all the shots" and has all the power. Giving up attachment is the price of freedom and contentment.

This kind of renunciation or detachment is not possible until one sorts out (discriminates/viveka) the distinction between what is Eternal and what is non-eternal. Constant reflection on this, and study of the dharma scriptures with an authentic teacher, reveals a myriad ways to think on this. If something is Eternal, then it is timeless, which means it is beyond space, which means It is indivisible, and that means It is all there is. As the Indian rishis realized, then, there is the changing Eternal (finite manifestations of Reality) and the Unchanging Eternal. The sages and philosophers started delineating these changing manifestations — the elements, the body, its energy, the mind and ego. In precise detail these are laid out for us so that, like a stalk of grass, we can pull away the sheaths from the very innermost core, the unchanging Essence, which they realized as Existence-Awareness-Bliss Absolute.

Further, renunciation is not condemnation (or rejection), but deification. Seeking out that Eternal, under proper guidance, reveals *"That One who is the Eternal in all noneternal things, the Intelligence of the intelligent, who though ever One and Unchanging fulfills the desires of the many."* Thus, thinking in this way, earthly life vibrates with Peace, Freedom, and Blessedness.

Thus does the difference between a successful earthly life and a lifetime lived in samsara reveal its divine secret.

---

## From Eshanatrayam to "Dharmatrayam"

**Those living under the limitations of the Eshanatrayam assume:**
- The world is the only reality
- We are separate individuals that are born and die; I am my body, emotions, thoughts, personality, ego…
- The purpose of life is pleasure; my home is for security and entertainment; my wealth is for me and mine
- My spouse is there for my happiness and fulfillment
- Children are physical bodies and personalities that are brought forth to fulfill my earthly desires
- Karmas and samskaras (tendencies) developed over lifetimes do not exist

**In contrast, householder yogis proceed on the following principles:**
- Only Brahman/God is Real; the world is a manifestation of Its dynamic power, maya; it deludes when discrimination is absent; it is sportive play when discrimination and detachment are present
- The Atman (Self/Soul) is never born or dies but associates with psycho-physical forms
- The purpose of life is to realize the Self; one's home is an ashram and wealth is to support noble causes, dharma, and raising a dharmic family
- One's spouse is a divine companion, of transcendent Essence, to have and to hold, with selfless loving service, along the path of Yoga
- Children are so many forms of the one indivisible Atman temporarily in one's care to help them pick up the thread of Yoga from previous lifetimes
- The manifestation of innate tendencies (samskaras) are to be scrutinized with guidance from the preceptor in order to nurture the beneficial and help neutralize the negative

◆ BABAJI BOB KINDLER

# INTRODUCING GODBLOGS
## "Brahman-Bytes" in the Aftermath of the Avatar's Descent

On SRV Association's new membership website, srvwisdom.org, a fresh philosophical phenomenon is taking place. Under the sub-heading "Brahman Bytes," concise but deep teachings are being rendered, utilizing great sayings of illumined seers throughout time, particularly centering around verbal transmissions from the Avatars of world religions. Specific sayings from Sri Ramakrishna, Swami Vivekananda, and Sarada Devi are heading the row, as Their teachings apply so well to both the insights and problems of today's spiritual seekers. In this short article, several prime examples are presented, to give the reader a brief glimpse of the dozens of "Godblogs" beings posted monthly to assist the practitioner in that most crucial art of inner contemplation.

### The Fullness of Emptiness
*I may have no Substance, but I have Essence.*

One day at the circus, a discarded balloon got to talking with some cast away, half-eaten cotton-candy. It complained to its unusual partner that, though it looked full, it always felt empty, and admitted that for some reason it had always loved dullness and had a real dread of sharp things. Commiserating in

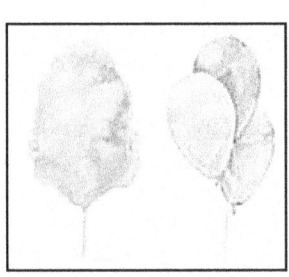

turn, the cotton-candy offered back, that though its persona looked confident and colorful, it really just evaporated immediately when people came near; and further, that it had a hidden fear that it possessed no real substance whatsoever. At that moment in the cathartic conversation, a passing elephant moving through the circus grounds stepped on the both of them. Some floating soap bubbles blown from a toy pipe by a child's breath looked down over the pathetic scene, and witnessed all of this inconsequential phenomena.

Emptiness, *shunyata*, and fullness, *purnyata*, are a very special pairs of opposites. Like form and formlessness, and bondage and liberation (but unlike happiness and sorrow and pleasure and pain), they require close contemplation by spiritual aspirants who desire to reach the Ultimate Goal of spiritual life, called Enlightenment. Such deep ruminations upon Divine Reality are far beyond the side-show arenas where physically-oriented hatha yoga, health-obsessed food-faddism, ego-posturing kirtan displays, and weakness-promoting psycho-therapy, set up their big-tent carnival acts and revivals. Spiritual life is mostly about building character, the luminaries have told us, not about sensationalism, sensuality, mystery-mongering, and cultural compromises.

The world of name and form in time and space is unreal; as hollow as bamboo. In brief, objects will not satisfy; senses will never become satiated; human relations will never fulfill; a Utopian society will never occur — it is all a complete myth. *"The One remains, the many change and pass. Heaven's Light forever shines, Earth's shadows fly; Life, like a dome of many-colored glass, stains the white radiance of Eternity."*

So choose. There is the worthless, balloon-like emptiness of a purposeless existence burdened by all manner of worries and sufferings, or the Ecstatic Emptiness of the pristine Mind stripped clean of all burdens and objects by God-realization. There is the uncomfortable, over-bloated cotton-candy-like fullness with its lavishly-abundant excesses and pseudo-religious indigestion, or the heady, exhilarating Fullness of all-inclusive Oneness that adamantly affirms, *"All is Brahman."* As the Great Swami Vivekananda has declared, in his *"wisdom is compassion"* way:

*"Gold and silver have I none, but what I have I give to thee freely, and that is the knowledge of the goldness of gold, the silverness of silver, the manhood of man, the womanhood of woman, and the reality of 'Everything is the Lord!' And that this Lord we are trying to realize from time without beginning in the objective, and in the attempt, throwing up such 'queer' creatures of our fancy as man, woman, child, body, mind, earth, sun, moon, stars, the world, love, hate, property, wealth, etc.; also ghosts, devils, angels, and gods, God, etc. Herein lies the secret. Says Patanjali, the father of Yoga: 'When a man rejects all the superhuman powers, then he attains the raincloud of virtues.' He sees God. He becomes God, and helps others become the same."*

### Think Small
*Essence of Objects, Savor of the Senses, Matter of the Mind*

A *tanmatra* is tiny increment of mental material. As such, it is a mote of thought, a spark of intelligence. As mind projects thoughts into objects, unseen by souls stuck in the illusion of time, tanmatras transform themselves into all manner of particles on earth, i.e., pollen in the air, bursts of flavor on the tongue, grains of sand on the beach, wafts of fragrance on the wind, etc. Tanmatras are also the vibrating minutia of internal experiences in dream. Swami Vivekananda pointed out that Western society, and

the modern world in general, has overlooked or forgotten these tiny sources in the mind's vast arsenal of powers — in some cases for centuries, in other cases, since the "beginning."

The result of forgetfulness concerning what is infinitesimal, and smaller, has resulted in many broken connections — not only between mankind and nature, but more essentially, between natural life, outer life, and internal life. In nature, the sun emits particles of warmth and light via its rays into the earth's atmosphere. In the outer life of body and senses, the blood carries particles of nourishment along vessels to the various organs of action and knowledge. In inner life, the psychic prana carries particles of experiential knowledge through subtle channels to the individual, collective, and cosmic mind. Thus, changing particles, from atoms to ideas, are enacting life on all levels of existence. All "particle theories" are incomplete if they do not provide for the presence of, or even a glimpse of, the tanmatras.

And what to speak of the light emitting from a single sun, halcyon light from celestial bodies — not just planets in space, but angelic bodies in heavenly realms — are exuding tanmatras continually. On earth, even, the human body is casting off and radiating a multitude of these minute specks and sparks, from skin cells to drops of moisture to emotional vibrations to the engaging scintilla of invigorating vital force flowing from the eyes. As Vivekananda says it, "....we all throw out these tanmatras, just as a flower continuously sends out fine particles which enable us to smell it." He sends us deeper, looking for their mixed indications, however, when he states: "Every day we throw out a mass of good and evil; all the atmospheres are full of these minute materials."

Whether called a halo, an aura, or *ojas*, to see only the outer spectacle without knowing its tiny sources is to remain unaware of these pervasive living particles. The knowers of Divine Reality do "think big" in their expressions and evaluations of the inner and outer cosmos, but arrive at these marvelous mental insights by "thinking small" in the interim. AUM, Peace, Peace....Peace be unto all particles!

## I "Shutter" to Think About It
*The Wood of Worldliness & the Glass of Godliness*

Sri Sarada Devi, supplicated as the "Holy Mother" by Her millions of precious spiritual children, has specified the difference between awakened and unawakened souls here on earth by using a simple teaching from nature. At one time, She was heard to say that *"Lightning flashes appear in the windowpane, but not in the wooden shutters."* Unless one has some grounding in the dharma, some knowledge of philosophy, or some familiarity with spirituality, this statement might "pass right over one's head," as the saying goes.

Though there may be several meanings to such a pregnant statement, one of them seems unmistakable in its import. Pertaining to people, it is a matter of their state of mind and intellect. In other words, is the mind thick, or transparent? If it is thick, like wood, then very little light (of intelligence) will reflect in it. The mental body itself will resist penetration. Glass on the other hand, will show up every particle of light passing in and through it, representing refined intelligence and the marvels of its presence in the awakened human being.

And there is also the case — though we "shutter" to think about it — of the windows that have had their shutters closed over it, and tightly fastened as well. This symbolizes minds that have completely turned away from the potential for higher awareness in the human being, and instead, focus upon all that is tainted by the darkness of root ignorance. Shutters as boundaries are one thing; shutters as coverings are another. The halcyon Light of pure, conscious Awareness may never visit the latter. As Lord Buddha stated when He was questioned about His teaching of the two kinds of living beings, i.e., awakened and unawakened:

*"You ask if there is a third type of being — those who are in the process of awakening? The answer is, that they are already awakened. Their minds are simply still in the process of realizing it."*

Thus, in brief: 1. shutters open but as yet still unreceptive to the Light, 2. shutters closed to completely block out all of the Light, or 3. the shutterless window pane itself that receives all of the Light, all of the time — the choices are listed. When it comes time to clean house, spiritually speaking, if the soul is reticent and declares, "I do not do windows," then a mere dusting of the shutters is about all that will ever happen. As Hastamalaka sings in his famous stotram:

*"Absolutely unique, the ineffable Essence which is the source and origin of all, the primal Purusha, playfully manifesting Itself in Pure Mind, Who is the one impartial sun, reflecting in the different water pots of various intellects, That One and I are identical, non-different, inseparable."*

## Like An Eskimo Studying Snow Conditions, Daily
*God Is All White Today*

Whatever the weather outdoors is like, most beings residing in the realms of name and form in time and space are living in the thick snow of desire for pleasure, simultaneously surrounded by the ever-encroaching snowbanks of pervasive suffering. A more sensitized awareness of the folly of such a lifestyle, however, could effectively take them all indoors and place them near the fireplace of fulfillment, surrounded by the satisfying warmth of inner peace.

For this positive change to occur, a study of the mind's awareness, day to day, using the method of meditation based in observational discernment (*vivekadhyan*) has to be undertaken for a time. As the changing conditions of the mind are perceived via this twin method, a desire for withdrawal (*vairagyam*) from all things that cycle and transition (*samsara*) comes upon the soul. When this state of mind is more fully matured, again, over time, the rare and special boon of detached Witness-Consciousness (*sakshi-bhutam*) arises, and the now peaceful spiritual adept simply watches and waits at the echelon of all phenomena — like an eskimo sitting in the doorway of his igloo and, for his own highest good, and that of his family and his tribe — observing even the slightest change in snow conditions all around him.

The hypnotist in the therapist's office holds up a shining metal object and tells the patient to "Watch the watch; watch the watch." The patient falls into a deep revery, identifying with the flow of dredged-up memories, thinking they are real. The dehypnotist in the guru's ashram holds forth the *japa mala* and tells the aspirant, "Watch the mind; watch the mind." The aspirant soon becomes a luminary, as the cold snow of root ignorance (*mulavidya*) melts away in the blissful, transcendental sunshine of burgeoning Nondual Awareness.

— *For more Godblogs go to srvwisdom.org*

◆ *Roshi Hogen Bays*

# DO NOT WORRY: NATURE IS DOING JUST FINE

The Whole of Life is just fine. And, as a culture and as individuals we are worried. Climate change, political upheaval, pollution, ethnic conflict, and health crises can weigh upon our hearts and minds. We worry we are doing something wrong. We are anxious that if only we were more skillful, more ethical, more wise, more heart centered — the world, our society and we, would be saner, safer and healthier. In Reality all these worries are unnecessary. The whole world, and all it contains, is just fine as it is. But if everything is ok, why does it seem so wrong and what is appropriate action?

**The Illusion of Separateness**

Separation is the root of anxiety. One of the proper functions of a human brain is to discriminate one thing from another. It is helpful to be able to know the difference between a door and a wall, but to view doors as separate from walls is wrong. In the same way our lives are a small part of nature herself.

When we imagine there are two things: nature, and we who inhabit nature, this gives rise to the illusion that there is a conflict between the natural activity of Nature, and we humans who are damaging it. This illusion has gelled into the deeply held belief that we are a separate species beyond the natural world.

When we feel separate, we begin defining and defending personal territory; "this is mine, not yours." We dream that we can make what is "mine" to be always safe and warm. We develop an unconscious hope for a Utopia; a frozen belief of safety in a world without conflict, disease, destruction or death. We can then imagine we can control the world and wield power over such things as carbon dioxide, governments, and gluten. We imagine that if we just did things right, we would be free from suffering. This confusion about reality has led us to believe we have overwhelming and hopeless problems.

**The Myth of Human Superiority**

At a gross level, we humans are a force of nature just as volcanos, hurricanes, and typhoons are. We are a part of the ebb and flow of the Whole, just as birth, activity, and death are. We humans create, adjust, and ponder. Beavers make dams, wasps make nests, and humans make condominiums, sometimes very complex ones. Just because we can make cell phones, we think we are superior and special. It is the mind of separation, superiority, and specialness that creates obstacles. When we think they are real, we become desperate to solve the obstacles we created. To what end? A longer life? More trouble?

**The Arrogation of our Thoughts**

On an intimate level, our separation and subsequent problems are the result of believing our thoughts. Why do we 'think' we are in control of our thoughts? Paying attention, we find an endless stream of images, ideas, and sensations we have no control over. Why do we believe we are the originator of thought when we never know what is going to pop into our minds next? Why do we believe that the thoughts we think are true? Why do we believe that there is even a thinker of thoughts? We assume we have answers to these questions despite all the evidence to the contrary. Thoughts just arise from the mysterious source at the root of life

But this tendency towards separation is not another problem to be solved. It too is part of the dynamic swirling "is-ness" of the Whole! To see the Whole and not get lost in the parts is one of the steps of spiritual practice. In my tradition the first steps are to ground our awareness in the body of this moment, to allow the thinking mind to settle and then to turn the impersonal mind of awareness on everything.

**Authentic Independent Thought**

Everything we think of as "real" can be examined. This examination is very intimate and very personal. Each belief we hold can be scrutinized and inquired into. Do I really know this is true? We could start with the stories in the media and ask "is what I am seeing the whole truth?" Might there be other interpretations, other views, other sides, things left out or things not known that could also be equally true? We can turn our curious attention to our relationships, our condition in the world, to anything. We are not intending any particular outcome, other than to know the whole truth. It is the Truth that sets us free.

This is the beginning of the investigation. There are two very important steps to take: inquiring into the most intimate question of all, "what am I?" What is it that is alive right here right now? What knows "thought?" And, how do I act? Where does love express itself? This is not a cold heartless universe, but one filled with swirling life. To answer these questions, being clear about the truth of Wholeness is most important.

Roshi Hogen Bays is an elderly Zen practitioner who lives at Great Vow Zen Monastery in Oregon.

JEFFREY ROTHMAN

# THE RELATIONSHIP BETWEEN JUDAISM & THE SPIRITUAL TECHNOLOGIES OF INDIA

Any intelligent person can observe that a primary theme which characterizes our current historical age is an unstoppable trend toward global unity. Like all trends in the world of change, or Maya, this inescapable trajectory has a dual aspect that a wise person recently described as the difference between "unity in conformity" and "unity in diversity." "Unity in conformity" is the attempt to blot out all differences between cultures to create a single monolithic culture, whereas "unity in diversity" is the more spiritually evolved understanding that, while we all share the same Divine Essence, this Essence expresses Itself in unique ways through the multifaceted subcultures of humanity.

In the domain of religion, the relationship between Judaism and the spiritual technologies of India is a good test case for successfully implementing this principal of unity in diversity. Before explaining why I believe that advanced methods of meditation discovered in India can be thought of as technologies, and before commenting on why I believe that the spiritual technologies of India can successfully be imported into a religion like Judaism, let me first say a few words about what makes Judaism unique as a religion. As Ramakrishna taught, all religions share the overarching goal of God-Realization, yet each one has a unique approach to worship and ritual that should be maintained and respected.

One primary aspect that makes Judaism unique as a religion is its extreme loyalty to formless monotheism, a strict and limited approach to worship that is arguably only shared by Islam. The absolute oneness of God is affirmed in the Torah, which says, *"Hear, o Israel, Jehovah is our God, Jehovah is One"* (Deuteronomy 6:4). The Jewish prohibition against all forms of image worship is a unique addition to this teaching of God's oneness, and is expressed in the first two of the Ten Commandments of the eternal Torah which say, *"I am Jehovah your God, who brought you out of Egypt, the land of slavery. You shall have no gods besides me. You shall not make for yourself an image in the form of anything in heaven above or on the earth beneath or in the waters below. You shall not bow down to worship them"* (Exodus 20:4).

The view that God is ultimately one existed in other religions before Judaism, and is expressed in religious texts like the Vedas that are even older than the Torah. The view that there is one God, but that the worship of dualistic images is nevertheless permitted, is not the same as the Jewish conception of monotheism. Furthermore, exclusive devotion to one deity (henotheism) has always existed in human religious experience, such as when it spontaneously manifested during the famous reign of the Pharaoh Akhenaten who devoted himself exclusively to the Sun God in defiance of Egyptian norms. However, the Jewish combination of exclusive devotion to the one God, the command that other gods are to be completely ignored by the devotees of Jehovah, the strong emphasis that God is formless, and the complete abolition of all image worship was something unique and unprecedented in human history.

While many more qualifications are probably necessary to explain Judaism's unique approach to worship, it can be said in short that a religious Jew who ignores these central precepts of the Torah by worshipping images has abandoned a core principal of the Jewish religion. This unique approach to worship (also shared with Islam) does not imply that the Jewish approach to worship is superior to other religions, only that it is different. A devotee who worships the image of Krishna or Kali with their whole heart as their highest ideal will reach the same goal of God-Realization as a Jew who wholeheartedly meditates on Jehovah. However, the shared goal and underlying essence that Judaism and Vedic religion share do not negate surface differences that make them unique as religions.

### The Blessing of Holding Two Ideals at Once

With these preliminary statements about Judaism in mind, a question naturally arises for the modern spiritual practitioner who worships as a Jew but also desires to partake of India's priceless spiritual offerings: Can I stay faithful to the Jewish religion while practicing meditation techniques that originated in India? For me, this question is not merely theoretical, but pragmatic. As a religious Jew, practicing "Eastern" meditation techniques has been a crucial part of my spiritual life. I also happen to believe that the meditation methods originally discovered in India are the most potent tools for accelerating spiritual development that humanity currently possesses. They are not mere rituals of a foreign religious tradition, but actual spiritual technologies that can radically accelerate the process of God-Realization for any person in any religion. For this reason, they are not only relevant to the traditions they emerged from, but have a universal purpose connected to the salvation of collective humanity. In this article, I intentionally use the term "Meditation Technologies of India," because the salvific methods that emerged from India cannot be limited to a single religious system.

To be clear, I am not saying that India is the only culture to discover meditation technologies, or that all spiritual methods that happen to come from India are necessarily effective. I am also not claiming that India's religious culture is perfect. I am merely claiming that, in my opinion, and for reasons fully known only to God, the most advanced spiritual technologies of meditation available today originated in India. By "advanced," I am referring to the fact that these meditation methods have been proven to consistently produce life altering enlightenment experiences in people who practice them over time.

### India's Unique Meditation Techniques

Speaking from experience, I can only personally report on the value of Buddhist meditation, for this is the only method I have deeply engaged in over long periods of time with actual teachers. My limited exposure to India's plethora of religious offerings does not negate the fact that India has graced the world with many other equally potent meditative systems and techniques, such as the yogic meditation methods taught by Krishna in the Bhagavad Gita and Patanjali in the Yoga Sutras, merely to name two of many more. While the West has only begun to discover this treasure trove of spiritual technologies, India has faithfully preserved them for untold thousands of years in a series of remarkably ancient lineages. More recent iterations of these lineages find expression in works like the Bhagavad Gita and the Buddhist Sutras, but thousands of years before Krishna taught yogic meditation to the world, and thousands of years before Buddha taught his techniques of meditative concentration, the sage Rama was initiated into similar yogic methods by luminaries like Vasishtha. Before Rama's generation, who can even calculate the antiquity of India's priceless spiritual offerings that have only recently been discovered by the West?

To exhaust the list of India's blessed spiritual lineages would be impossible here, but my few examples will hopefully suffice to make my general argument that the spiritual technologies of India should be thought of as Indian or Vedic schools and not strictly Buddhist or "Hindu." And though they are the offerings of India, they are simultaneously significant for all humanity. Just as a scientific discovery like the light bulb transcends its cultural origins, and is eventually dispersed to people of all cultures, so scientific meditation technologies like Buddha's mindfulness practices or Krishna's timeless methods of yogic concentration can be utilized by people of all religions, even if they happen to be discovered by people of a foreign religion. As religious people, we must acknowledge the plain fact that the most effective methods of meditation in existence today come from India. For the age has finally dawned when, at the command of God, these techniques are being dispersed globally to assist in the collective awakening of the human race.

If God-Realization is the universal goal of all religions, it would be foolish for any spiritual seeker to ignore the technologically superior spiritual methods of India, just as it would be foolish for a nation's leader to ignore the existence of superior water purification technology just because it happened to be discovered by another nation. The predictable hesitancy of some religious Jews to import India's meditation techniques into their own tradition is regrettable but also understandable, for these spiritual technologies happened to be discovered in a religious culture that includes image worship. Additionally, the Buddhist tradition generally ignores the idea of a personal God altogether, and to an outsider's perspective can seem atheistic.

### Specifying Different Forms of Worship

I believe that a harmony can be embodied between the two extremes of Jewish traditionalism and general human spiritual evolution. Like all the Jewish prophets in the Bible, I wholeheartedly agree that a religious Jew who engages in any form of image worship has violated the commandments of the Torah I shared above, and any Jew who advocates such practices for other religious Jews should be considered to be a false prophet. What I am arguing is that one can simply practice the method itself without engaging in foreign forms of worship. The method can successfully be extracted from the religious tradition it happened to emerge from, and can be imported into another religious tradition like Judaism without diminishing the essence of either. For instance, to practice daily Buddhist meditation and

> "....the most advanced spiritual technologies of meditation available today originated in India; these meditation methods have been proven to consistently produce life altering enlightenment experiences in people who practice them over time."

to attend Buddhist retreats does not require a person to renounce their belief in a Personal God, to worship the Buddha, or to forfeit their Jewish identity. To practice the universal methods of Yoga or Vedanta does not necessarily require a Jew to bow to an image of Shiva or Vishnu, or to violate the ritualistic commandments of the Torah in any way.

It can be argued that the scientific revolution attained its most refined form of expression in Europe, but that a person does not need to embrace all aspects of Western culture to benefit from these discoveries. Issac Newton happened to be an Englishman and a Christian, but his discoveries are universally significant and have been utilized by people of all cultures. Similarly, the Buddha, Patanjali, and Krishna happened to be products of Vedic culture, but their methods of meditation can be practiced by people of any culture to reduce suffering and to enhance the probability of mystical experience.

### Remaining True to the Tradition

It should also be said that while there is a danger in completely ignoring the meditation techniques of India, there is also a danger in extracting from them only the aspects we prefer. Utilizing the Buddha's mindfulness methods for stress reduction alone, while ignoring his emphasis on ethics and the higher goal of Enlightenment, is an example of making Buddhism or mindfulness "in our own image," and would almost certainly violate the historical Buddha's personal wishes. Similarly, using ancient yogic meditation techniques exclusively to "manifest my

> "Utilizing the Buddha's mindfulness methods for stress reduction alone, while ignoring his emphasis on ethics and the higher goal of Enlightenment, is an example of making Buddhism or mindfulness "in our own image," and would almost certainly violate the historical Buddha's personal wishes. Similarly, using ancient yogic meditation techniques exclusively to "manifest my desires," a sad fad in some New Age communities, is a spiritually harmful absurdity similar to using the teachings of Jesus merely to become wealthy."

desires," a sad fad in some New Age communities, is a spiritually harmful absurdity similar to using the teachings of Jesus merely to become wealthy. I am not saying we should remake these traditions as we see fit; only that a balance must be struck that adapts these ancient spiritual methods to the needs of the modern world and to members of other religions without compromising their essential principals. Religious Jews who desire God-Realization should attempt to stay true to both our traditional Jewish modes of worship, and the underlying philosophical principals of these Indian or Vedic methods simultaneously.

This balance is subtle and difficult to strike, especially for Jews. As Jews, we must avoid allowing Eastern religions to entice us into foreign modes of worship that the Torah clearly forbids, but should also never take the view that our way of worship is superior. For instance, a religious Jew who desires to follow the Torah could practice the yogic techniques advocated by Swami Vivekananda, but should not worship the image of the Divine Mother Kali as he often did. They should also simultaneously understand that the God-Realization embodied by Vivekananda is the same God-Realization embodied by Jewish masters like Jesus, the Jewish Messiah, who worshipped the Personal God in a Jewish style. One can say that a violin master and a piano master are both musical masters, but that they merely choose to express this mastery through different mediums. Similarly, a Jewish master and a master who worships the image of Kali both share the same identical Essence, but merely express this Essence through the modality of a different tradition.

Sri Ramakrishna himself demonstrated that God-Realization can be experienced through both Vedic and Muslim styles of worship, but also found he could not worship at the Kali temple when practicing the strict monotheism of Islam which is comparable to Judaism. While identical in Essence, he arguably showed that the unique ritualistic ethos of specific traditions should nevertheless be maintained. He embodied the principal of unity in diversity, revealing that the subtle distinctions among faiths on the surface do not negate their shared goal and shared Essence.

### Is My Religious Perspective Narrow?

On the other hand, this desire to maintain the distinctiveness of Judaism can go too far. A Jew who ignores the spiritual technologies of India because they are afraid of violating the Torah is comparable to a Jew who was commanded by God to travel to the other side of the world. In his stubbornness, he said, "Because Jews did not invent the airplane, and because airplanes were never mentioned by Moses in the Torah, I refuse to use one." He then spent months walking across land, and boating across the sea, but died before he reached his destination. His journey could have been so much easier and speedier if he had only humbled himself and used an airplane! Similarly, the Jew makes a serious error who thinks, "Because Vedic worshippers discovered meditation, I could never use it." It will take this Jew far longer to reach the goal of God-Realization than God Himself intended. For the many thousands of lifetimes naturally required for the average person to fully realize God-Consciousness can be expedited to a few, or even to one, with the help of a potent method of meditation.

I hope and pray that the promotion of authentic meditation technologies from India is embraced by worldwide Jewry as the centuries unfold. Narrow-minded Jews have always resisted integrating wisdom from other cultures into Judaism, failing to see that Judaism is dynamic, not static. Integrating wisdom from other cultures is not the same as abandoning the core essence of the Torah. For while Judaism has a set of unmovable core principals, it also leaves room for the integration of outside wisdom. Many aspects of Babylonian, Egyptian, and Near Eastern culture were integrated into Judaism as it first emerged as a distinct religion. Similarly, concepts from the Zoroastrian tradition found their way into Judaism at the time of the prophet Daniel. The great rabbis Maimonides and Philo both synthesized Greek wisdom with rabbinic theology. Many Kabbalists were influenced by Sufis and their iconoclastic mystical methods. The democratic ideals of America's founding fathers have influenced many developments in Judaism today. Judaism has been influenced by the wisdom of so many other cultures that to fully describe this process would take countless volumes.

From this perspective, the anything but novel idea that meditation practices and wisdom from India can successfully be imported into Judaism reminds me of Solomon's famous saying, *"There is nothing new under the sun."*

Jeffrey Rothman is an author, musician, and social worker who currently lives in Tulsa, Oklahoma. His books primarily concentrate on how to integrate spiritual practice into daily life. His writings and music can be found on:

www.jeffreyrothman.net.

◆ *Swami Sunirmalananda*

# THE SPECIAL ESOTERIC SIGNIFICANCE OF SARASVATI & HER VEENA
## Sacred Vibration as Emanation from the Goddess

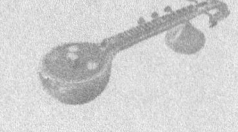

Swami Vivekananda narrates a vision-like dream he had once. He saw Sri Ramakrishna. From Sri Ramakrishna's heart sprang forth a huge brilliant ball of light. From that light burst forth Mother Sarasvati with her Veena. She started playing her Veena. With the notes sprang forth animals, birds, trees, plants, mountains, everything. She stopped playing and everything returned to her Veena, slowly. She then transformed herself into that ball of light. That ball of light then entered Sri Ramakrishna's heart.

This was a glorious vision. Veena as an instrument is considered to be one of the oldest stringed instruments with a perfect sound-producing capability. The others, like sitar, sarod, etc., which you see being played everywhere, were subsequent. There is an inseparable connection between Mother Sarasvati and the Veena. It's heavy, but She chose this instrument over the others. Sri Krishna has the flute.

Amazingly enough, Sarasvati, also called Sâradâ, does not hold any weapon, like Lakshmi. She just has her Veena and sometimes a book. The most significant form of Sarasvati, presented to humanity, is her Veena-holding form, with a swan as her vehicle. In passing, Hindu thinkers since ages knew that all life is sacred and important. So they intelligently placed different animals with different deities — the snake, the elephant, nothing but pure vibration. You strike a drum. The drum will have no effect on anything or anyone if there is no medium to convey the vibrations of the strike. Air is the absolutely essential medium for vibrations to go from one end to another. So when you strike a drum, the drum's skin vibrates, leading to the vibration compressing and releasing the air around, and thus moving further on. These air vibrations affect the hair follicles in the ears, and we say we hear the drum. It's all vibration.

The same with what we see also. The so-called solid universe, with its solid mountains and rivers, are all nothing but vibrations. An apple looks black lying on the ocean bed, but it is brilliant red on the surface of the earth. It is all reflection of rays and vibrations. The ocean is blue because it permits blue rays to penetrate as far down as possible and cancels out other wavelengths.

**The Subtle Source of Gross Vibrations**

What we see are wavelengths or reflections. What we hear are vibrations. So what are these solid things all around? Though these things look solid, as we were told since our school days, there is nothing solid there; it is all atoms. So we are seeing, hearing, and experiencing an illusion all the time. All around we have vibrations and we are lost amidst these vibrations completely, totally. What we call emotions — love, hate, etc. — are also vibrations, alone.

> "She started playing her Veena. With the notes sprang forth animals, birds, trees, plants, mountains, everything. She stopped playing and everything returned to her Veena, slowly."

cow, etc. — so that while venerating the deities, people understood that the animals too should be adored.

Sarasvati's Veena creating this universe and taking it back again into it is an extraordinary phenomenon. The Word becoming form, and the form returning to the Word again. Rather, it is the musical notes that become alive and return to their original state. There is a science about it in India and ancient Hindus discussed this science as sphota concept. Sphota is the bursting forth of sound vibrations which ultimately lead to the manifested universe. There is one thing to note here. Sarasvati's Veena is an instrument after all. It's inert, so to say. There is an Intelligent Divine behind the instrument, whose fingers makes things happen.

This leads us to the idea of vibrations. Everything comes out of vibrations, everything is in a state of vibration, and everything ends with the end of vibration. Sound, as we know, is

These vibrations originate from certain sources. Going backwards, these vibrations are traced to subtle pranic vibrations. Swami Vivekananda's extraordinary talks on Prana, as an introduction to his Raja Yoga lessons, are eyeopeners. He says that "Pran" means to vibrate. In the beginning there is just space, or what is. Then there is this vibration. As vibration begins, it manifests itself as name and form. All we see and experience is name and form. When did it start and when does it end? The ocean cannot be asked to stop its waves for awhile. The waves come and go constantly. If you want to see the ocean, stop concentrating on the waves. So too with this empirical creation. If you want to listen to the melody behind, stop listening to the tumult in front. This is the idea.

What we see as solid creation, what we love so much, what we die for, and what we wish to live eternally for, is all vibration. They are vibrations of different forms and wavelengths. And these vibrations have a source. That source isn't anything physical at all. It is something different. Personified, it becomes "god" or Ishvara. Non-personified, it is the root or source.

In this way, the whole manifest universe is vibration, and we, through our senses, perceive these vibrations.

The question is, are these sound vibrations or light waves or electromagnetic waves? The ocean can be a wave, a piece of solid ice, water, and so on. So also, the one source vibration can assume several forms. Whatever the form of vibration, ultimately it is all prana. The source of this pranic vibration is sound according to some schools, thought according to some others, and something different according to yet others. Whether this whole universe has come to be manifested due to sound or thought or something else, it is temporary or relative. Name and form are not permanent. What comes, has to go. What is, will become modified. So it is all a series of constantly changing patterns.

**Imagination to Envisionment**

Just imagine for a moment, that we are inside a web of patterns and colors, projected by some root vibrations, and we are trying constantly to catch some pattern which we hope will be everlasting. We would do better by trying to discover the source of these vibrations. Perhaps we eventually reach the Veena in this way. But the Veena is not the ultimate source. There is the Veena player. Further in, this Veena player, Mother Sarasvati, merges in supreme Light. And that Light merges in Sri Ramakrishna.

The point is: why worry about the changing patterns when we have the everlasting source at hand? Why waste our precious lives and time in trying to make the patterns permanent and struggle to extract what we think is happiness of them?

This, then, is to be our struggle. The same vibrations have been here since time immemorial. And the same medicine has been prescribed by various doctors, in various languages, to help us overcome the illusion of permanence in these things. To know things in the right perspective is knowledge. And the source of all knowledge is Sarasvati. Surrendering to Her brings peace. The struggle we undergo, life after life, in order to extract happiness from the world can be directed to the seeking of higher happiness in the Source of everything. This struggle becomes sweeter as days pass by, and there is always help and support. And in the end is the source of all manifestation. Swami Vivekananda's vision of the Veena-playing Mother asks us to turn back towards the Source. This is the ideal.

Swami Sunirmalananda is a sannyasin of the Ramakrishna Order, and the monk in-charge of the Vedanta Society of Holland. He is Swami Bhuteshanandaji's disciple. The Swami had the privilege of serving his guru for a decade before serving the Ramakrishna Order's centers in Brasil and Geneva.

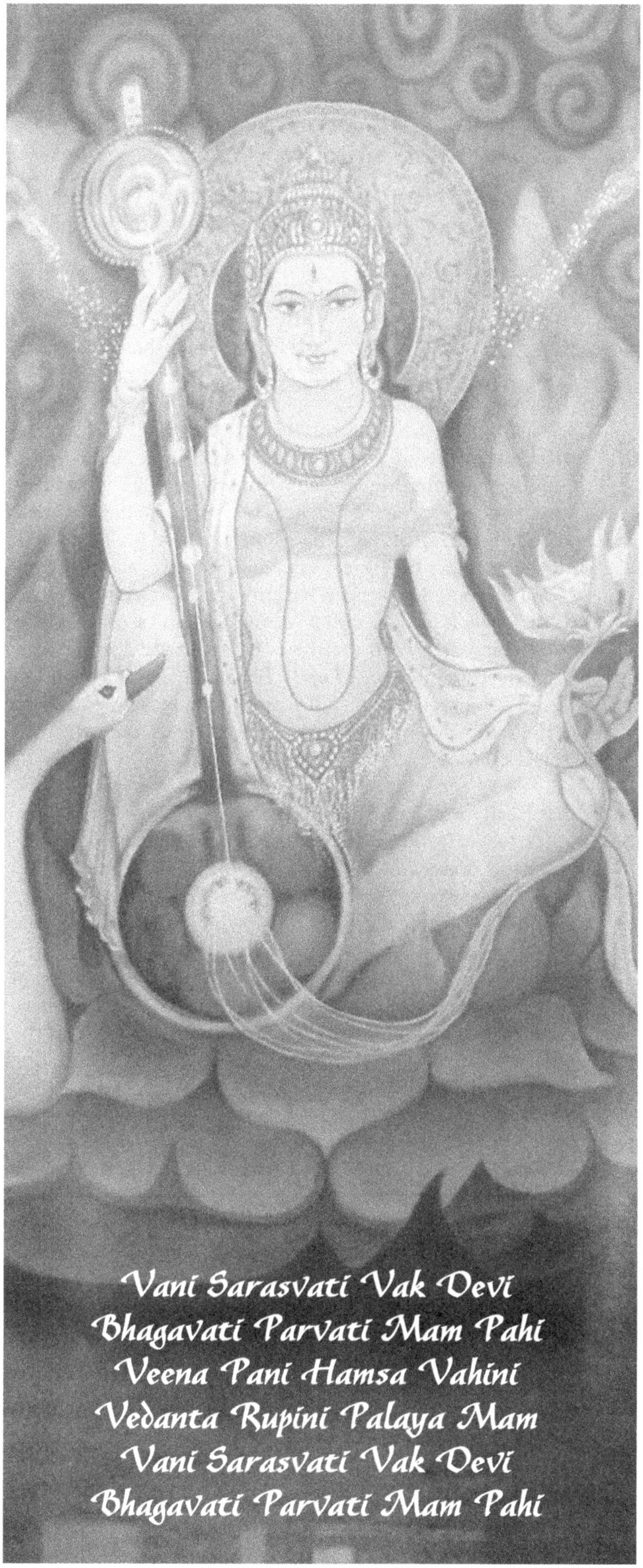

*Vani Sarasvati Vak Devi*
*Bhagavati Parvati Mam Pahi*
*Veena Pani Hamsa Vahini*
*Vedanta Rupini Palaya Mam*
*Vani Sarasvati Vak Devi*
*Bhagavati Parvati Mam Pahi*

◆ Brother Tadrupa

# INSTRUCTIONS ALONG THE PATH OF NONORIGINATION
## According to the Bhagavad Gita

Ajativada, nonorigination, is the essential axiom and spiritual discipline of the Advaita Vedanta Philosophy. "No birth, no death" sounds so simple to the novice truth seeker, but to grasp this principle to its fullest extent is to realize the profundity and fullness of Advaita (Nonduality) Itself. From the highest state of Consciousness, Ajativada is realized to be the all-inclusive Truth. Additionally, this pillar of eastern thinking is also inferred in other Indian darshanas (paths of clear seeing) such as Tantra, Pantajali's Yoga, and Buddhism. But as spiritual aspirants, how do we incorporate such a comprehensive teaching in an accessible way that frees the mind from unnecessary suffering and attachment? Sri Krishna's *Bhagavad Gita*, with its many yogas and seemingly infinite teachings, shows us the way. In this article, I will discuss how ajativada is interspersed in the Bhagavad Gita as a hands-on and masterful sequence of instructions that prepare Arjuna to win the spiritual battle in the mind and progress along the path of self-realization.

**What Really was Arjuna's Problem?**

It's very easy to think that Arjuna's predicament on the battlefield of Kurukshetra was due to simple human dearness and love of his relatives. On the surface, his hesitation was one of conventional love and attachment for his grandsire, Bhishma, and his archery guru, Drona, and other virtuous beings in the opposing army. What sane person would not feel some aversion to fighting their own family and favorite teacher? However, if we look at Arjuna's mind, we can see a distortion or covering of the truth of Ajativada. In short, Arjuna's fear of eliminating Bhishma and Drona is rooted in the idea that things are actually born and actually die, and the latter means they will never exist again. He believes their birth was a unique event in time and space, never to occur again, like the appearance and extinction of a species in the biological sense. Once they are gone, they are gone forever. Thus, to understand Arjuna's *vishada* (dejection) one must plumb deeper to the very root ignorance that beings harbor about the nature of the Universe, the Self, Reality, and the relationship between these. It's a problem of the obscuration of Self-knowledge due to desire, aversion, and attachment. And in terms of Patanjali's Yoga, Arjuna suffers *bhrantidarshana* (false-seeing) and *kleshas* (obstacles) as a result. His issue with nobly slaying his kinsmen is merely a symptom of a much deeper problem.

Arjuna's ignorance and mental state can be inferred, and more importantly, Sri Krishna's initial instructions on ajativada are contained in various slokas in the second chapter of the Bhagavad Gita. Below is a sampling:

*(2:12-13) Nor I, nor you, nor any of these ruling princes was ever non-existent before; nor is it that we shall ever cease to be in the future. As the indweller in the body experiences childhood, youth, and old age in the body, he also passes on to another body. The serene one is not affected thereby.*

*(2:16) The unreal has no existence, the real never ceases to be. The truth about both has been realized by the seers of divine principles.*

*(2:20) The Atman is neither born nor does it die. Coming into being and ceasing to be do not take place in It. Unborn, eternal, and changeless, it not killed when the body is slain.*

Sri Krishna seems to span various avastas (stages of growth) along the way of ajativada here. In every sloka, He emphasizes that there is something outside of the birth and death process, but from various levels of awareness as may be the case for the student's mind. The first stage, mentioned in 2:12-13, is for bound beings like Arjuna, who is attached to the body and senses, living at the physical plane only. He asks Arjuna to make an accessible micro-shift in his understanding in order to effect some degree of mental equanimity. This was the perfect instruction, given the immensity and immediacy of the horrible battle Arjuna is about to face. In essence, Sri Krishna says in the slokas, "Go ahead and believe in this diverse universe and beings, just remember there is an immortal inner traveler from body to body."

Sloka 2:16 is a well know verse dense with wisdom. Due to its esoteric meaning, it must have peaked Arjuna's interest when heard from Sri Krishna. The key Sanskrit word in this sloka is *tattvadarshibih*. This means one who is a seer of the *tattvas*, the various principles of the Cosmos. These tattvas sprout and then return, in an interconnected fashion, from seeds in the Cosmic Mind. In other words, this pregnant sloka implies a non-originated divine Yoga at the essence of all in the realm of appearances. It goes beyond the instruction in 2:12-13, by urging Arjuna to contemplate a relatedness between all aspects of the Universe, and also what is beyond. Sri Krishna instructs Arjuna to try to see this unity as the substratum of the apparent diverse entities. The Lord greatly expands on this unity in later chapters of the Gita. Lastly, Sri Krishna states the knowers of the Truth know the *tattvas*, the unreal or changeable, as well as the real and unchanging Reality.

In sloka 2:20, we see Sri Krishna seems to instruct from yet another higher level of awareness. He explains how when one is fully identified with the Atman, the Reality associated with limiting sheaths, the notions of birth, death, and transformation are not seen. This Atman-beatitude negates any secondary principles and borders on the final stage of realizing nonorigination.

If we look at Sri Krishna's overall framework in the slokas mentioned above, we can see He is schooling Arjuna's mind in ajativada via the Three Stages of Indian Philosophy. The first stage is Dualism, where the seeker sees the diversity of the universe and its beings as being actual, as opposed to apparent separation from God. The second stage, Qualified Nondualism, the seeker sees the universe and its being as an interdependent qualification of Reality that will ultimately be involved back into It. In the third stage, Nondualism, the seeker and the Universe are totally merged as a singular Reality. If they are aware of the world, it is seen as a mere appearance, like one who perceives a mirage knowing the desert as the true landscape. Thus we can see that Sri Krishna's plan follows the classic steps to higher knowledge outlined in several other scriptures, such as the Upanisads, to awaken Arjuna to the fullest comprehension of Divine Reality.

**Non-Origination & Sri Krishna's Method of Renouncing Action**

After giving the profound basics of ajativada, and thereby getting Arjuna off his knees and into higher curiosity, the immediate concern of how to perform actions and ultimately renounce them takes precedent for several chapters. Below are a series of slokas from chapters two, three, four, and five that help to reveal how non-origination is peppered throughout these yogas as the linchpin of the method of relinquishing action:

Sri Krishna instructs Arjuna in 2:49 to purify his actions via *buddhi yoga*, the path of realization through equanimity of intelligence. We hear the teaching of mental equipoise given over and over again in various spiritual paths and teachings. Yet, to activate and maintain this property of the mind is quite a mystery for some, especially when unexpected or unpleasant events arise in daily intercourse with the world. Lord Krishna solves this issue by providing us with a series of teachings, based in ajativada, to clarify and infill our understanding of the Universe, the nature of action, and the eternal Self.

One of the key teachings of chapter three around action is called the Circle of Sacrifice. This teaching, which concludes in 3:15, points to a chain of causation and connectedness between the forces of nature, food, beings, and their ultimate non-originated source in the Transcendental Reality. To do work in awareness of this knowledge constitutes mature yajna (sacrifice). It's the perfect teaching for the moment for Arjuna, who is out of dejection, but still identified with the field of action, body, and senses. From this wisdom, he can start to have a more complete view of the realm of activity where he can see, even in an empirical sense, that the two armies and his enemies are part of the Circle, and thus be assured they will never die in their essence. How could something that has its origin in the Imperishable ever die?

Sri Krishna further clears Arjuna's intellect through the

> "....to understand Arjuna's *vishada* (dejection) one must plumb deeper to the very root ignorance that beings harbor about the nature of the Universe, the Self, Reality, and the relationship between these. It's a problem of the obscuration of Self-knowledge due to desire, aversion, and attachment. And in terms of the Patanjali's Yoga, Arjuna suffers *bhrantidarshana* (false-seeing) and *kleshas* (obstacles) as a result. His issue with nobly slaying his kinsmen is merely a symptom of a much deeper problem."

*(2:49) Motivated action is, O Dhanajaya, far inferior to that performed with equanimity of mind; take refuge in this buddhi yoga; wretched are the result seekers.*

*(3:15) Know karma (action) to have risen from the Veda, and the Veda from the Imperishable. The all-pervading Veda is, therefore, ever centered in Yajna (sacrifice).*

*(3:43) Thus knowing Him as superior to the intellect, restraining the self by the Self, slay, O mighty-armed, the enemy in the form of desire, difficult to overcome.*

*(4:6) Though I am unborn, imperishable and the Lord of beings, yet subjugating My Prakriti, I come into being by My own Maya.*

*(4:14) Nor do actions taint Me, nor is the fruit of action desired by Me. He who thus knows Me is not bound by action.*

*(4:15) Having known thus even the ancient seekers after freedom performed action; therefore do you perform actions, as did the ancients in the olden times.*

*(5:10) He who acts, abandoning attachment, dedicating his deeds to Brahman, is untainted by sin as a lotus leaf by water.*

teaching of inherent knowledge, desire as the obscurer of this, and the teaching of the Hierarchy of Creation which is completed in sloka 3:43. The Lord transmits to Arjuna the order of superiority from the senses, body, mind, ego, intellect, and Atman. The important point here is that the ego-self is controlled by the higher Self, through the intellect's resort to knowledge of the Self as detached, unborn, and thus transcendent of the lower principles in the Hierarchy. This instruction fleshes out what it means to practice in buddhi yoga as mentioned in 2:49 and later slokas in the *Bhagavad Gita*.

In chapter 4, Sri Krishna expounds on the nature of Ishvara, the personal God, as the ultimate example for truth-seekers to follow in the path of renunciation of action. In sloka 4:6, Sri Krishna, who represents the *Paramatman*, or supreme Soul, explains His mysterious and all-inclusive nature. In the description, the Reality is described as unborn and unchanging which, points again to ajativada and its co-axiom aparinama, or non-transformation, but also as the ruler over the universe of appearances. 4:15 further explains that in the Lord's apparent embod-

> "Lord Krishna encourages Arjuna to use knowledge of how Ishvara benignly works, as the example for how to embody the higher wisdom in all actions, and thus destroy them ultimately. This sacred emulation is one way in which the fire of self-knowledge may be utilized to effect neutralization followed by relinquishment of all actions. One becomes a 'master idler,' as some teachers describe."

iment, he never cultivates desire for actions or their results. Finally, in sloka 4:16, Lord Krishna encourages Arjuna to use knowledge of how Ishvara benignly works as the example for how to embody the higher wisdom in all actions and thus destroy them ultimately. This sacred emulation is one way in which the fire of Self-knowledge may be utilized to effect neutralization followed by relinquishment of all actions. One becomes a "master idler," as some teachers describe. As sloka 5:10 explains, the whole process culminates in an actor that is really no actor anymore since they have become transparent to all actions. The yogi's awakened intelligence, which facilitates unbroken awareness of the unborn nature of Reality, renders all karma colorless, leaving no residue. The seeker rises above divisions, cause and effect, time, and space through this remembrance. This is fencing with the two swords of action and knowledge as taught by Sri Ramakrishna.

**Approaching the Cosmic Form through Wisdom**

In chapters six through ten, Sri Krishna continues to expand Arjuna's mind with various ignorance-destroying teachings. He comes back again and again to ajativada — the unborn and transcendental nature of Reality. The Lord goes to great lengths to demonstrate that this Truth infills, connects, and supports all that is in the realm of appearances. Several slokas are placed below to illustrate the method:

*(7:6-7) Know that these two natures are the womb of all beings. I am the origin and dissolution of the whole universe. There is nothing whatsoever higher than Me, O Dhananjaya. All this is strung on Me, as rows of gems on a string.*

*(8:20) But beyond this unmanifested, there is yet another Unmanifested Eternal Existence which does not perish even when all existences perish.*

*(9:18) I am the Goal, the Supporter, the Lord, the Witness, the Abode, the Shelter, the Friend, the Origin, the Dissolution, the Foundation, the Treasurehouse, and the Seed Imperishable.*

The two natures in 7:6-7 refer to the eight-fold lower nature of beings which are the five senses, mind, intellect, and ego, and the higher nature of the life energy which animates all beings and the universe. We can see Sri Krishna is showing Arjuna how to be a knower of the tattvas as mentioned earlier in 2:16, but not for mere scientific understanding. The point is to show the connection back to the unborn source of the universe. 8:20 raises Arjuna's consciousness even further. This verse helps the seeker to view these two natures and see them merely as the manifested/unmanifested, otherwise known as the realm of appearances, and know that Reality is beyond coming and going and perceptibility of the senses, and thus beyond birth and death. Sloka 9:18, which is a minute sample of the excellent teachings from chapter nine, illustrates that Arjuna is being schooled to take everything he could possible think of in the universe and see how its basis and essence is the Supreme Reality. These slokas and their respective chapters show the comprehensive method of raising one's consciousness through a sequence of stages that culminate in the "Vision of the Cosmic Form." The Lord teaches Arjuna how to know the Self and Universe in totality, and as a result the relationship between these two. Non-origination is a key foundation throughout these teachings.

**Conclusion and Practical Tips**

This article has discussed many instructions along the path of ajativada according to the Bhagavad Gita. If looked at as a whole, we can see that to know the truth of ajativada is nothing short of realizing the comprehensive unity of Existence in all its aspects, phases, and modes. In other words, Reality is Yoga. The path towards this direct knowledge is a complete remodeling of one's mind and understanding. An important practical point, especially for the Western seeker, is that thousands of "failures" are to be expected. For an observant student, "failures" provide personal feedback and insight into the unwanted cracks in one's intelligence and spiritual discernment. Reviewing and meditating on Sri Krishna's (and other dharma) teachings is frequently advised. Also, hearing them from an exemplar who embodies the wisdom in their life is immensely helpful. But most importantly, we need to remember that this knowledge is our inherent Nature from which we are never separate. Taking refuge in this as a prime mental position leads to inner peace which naturally dissolves the obstacles that inevitably come along the path.

Brother Tadrupa Josh McDaniel is an initiated student of SRV Associations. He has studied with Babaji Bob Kindler for eight years. Tadrupa serves as an advisor to the SRV Board of Directors and assists with various activities such as classes, retreats, and secretarial duties. In his professional life, Tadrupa enjoys serving and coaching students as a college math instructor.

# The Qualified Mind
## The Perfect Guru/Shishya Relationship

Spiritual practitioners and those just entering spiritual life sometimes struggle with the idea of taking a teacher. Is a teacher really necessary? With all the teachings available online and in books and scriptures, why not do it on one's own? – a la DIY spiritual enlightenment? What is the role of the spiritual teacher? How does one find or recognize a true spiritual guide? Why can't I be my own spiritual guide since all knowledge lies within and the true Self of all beings is ever-illumined? During a recent question and answer period, this writer heard her teacher respond to just such a question: "Yes, you have to do it yourself and you have to have a guide to show you how." This encapsulates the entire issue, so let us break it down further.

### My Disguise, and Maya's Disguise

There are many spiritual seekers in the West who have a strong sense of independence and self-reliance. Whereas this could portend the ability to storm the gates of Ignorance/Avidya veiling one's true nature as eternal, ever-free, blissful Awareness, it is often combined with three obstacles: impatience; unconscious acceptance that matter is the reality and the Self is the body; and often, it must be admitted, not a small degree of arrogance or pride of one's limited knowledge. Self-Realization is not some common article available for instant gratification or a degree learned online. Root ignorance, Avidya, is disguised in a plethora of ways and manifests variously and ceaselessly as identification and preoccupation with our bodies, gender, age, emotions, moods, intellectual abilities or challenges, with occupations, pleasures and sorrows, life goals, relations with others, ad infinitum. It takes a highly qualified mind, usually aided by discipleship to an authentic and qualified teacher, to storm that gate of Avidya and *"cross over to the farther shore beyond all darkness."*

Patanjali, the Father of Yoga, reduces these diverse manifestations to the following five: Ignorance (from which all the others evolve out), egotism, attachment, aversion, and clinging to life/fear of death. If we analyze our thoughts and motivations, which are both conscious and unconscious, and the actions resulting from them, they will fall into one or more of these five. And that is just in our ordinary consciousness. Ignorance veils the inner, subtler regions of the mind, known as our subconscious at the grosser end and visionary states at the subtler. Most essentially, this Ignorance stands between beings and what Swami Vivekananda called the Superconscious state, which aligns with the nondual state of pure Awareness called nirvikalpa or asamprajnata samadhis, Turiya or Turiyatita, depending on the philosophical school. Ordinary consciousness (waking state) is directed by the contents of the subconscious (dream and causal states) containing the seeds of karma, the tendencies and habits from prior lifetimes (samskaras), and desire.

For an individual under the sway of all these, removing ignorance, egotism, attachment, aversion, and clinging to life is like trying to remove the salt already dissolved in a glass of water. One requires knowledge and tools to do this. However, before anything else, one needs to be aware that water (Soul) is actually sweet, pure, and refreshing by its nature, and not characterized by salt (phenomena with its pleasure and pain), and have the yearning to taste water free from salt. What would it be like to experience the Freedom of the Soul/Atman? To know one's birthless, deathless, infinite Self? To be free from all fear? Is it possible? The role of the teacher is to exemplify this inner Freedom, this communion with the Atman (true Self), and the mastery of mind and senses that attend upon these. Then, in addition to exemplifying peace of mind and freedom, the teacher explains the revealed scriptures and the methods that lead to self-mastery that eventually break the bonds of root ignorance, that is, if the student perseveres with right aspiration.

"Yet," some might respond, "The nondual scriptures and bygone sages tell us all this and lay out methods to follow. Why not simply do what they say? These are the great, eternal Teachers, the Aptavakyas, which means they are to be trusted and emulated with faith." Indeed, they are, but the real question is whether one properly understands their meaning, how to follow their methods, and how to understand the results of these practices, which vary with each individual's karma, samskaras (tendencies from prior births), and temperament (gunas). The ability to understand the import of their teachings is hindered by the very ignorance and its offshoots one needs to overcome. One's mind must be qualified, or one must take a living teacher who is qualified.

For example, a mind that is susceptible to the gunas will understand the scriptures and great Teachers with some clarity only as long as a cycle of sattva/balance is upon it. If rajas/restlessness is present, one will be distracted and unfocused, causing the teachings to be taken either in an incomplete or distorted fashion colored by one's desires and aversions. When tamas/dullness is present in the mind, a student may either fall asleep or conclude the teacher or scriptures are meaningless. Add to this the different karmas (apparently positive and apparently negative) arising in the spiritual aspirant's life, and the decision to take recourse only to non-embodied teachers of the past, or a great revealed scripture will be inadequate to find one's way. As Lord Vasishtha states in Vasishtha's Yoga, *"Trying to understand the scriptures without a teacher [embodied] is like trying to grow crops only at night."* Swami Vivekananda, in his book on Bhakti Yoga, explains the need of a Guru very clearly:

> "....students of Brahmajnan were expected to have control of their senses, tranquility of mind, the ability to forbear heat and cold without complaint. They had to have devotion to truth, nonviolence, gentleness of speech, and be willing to serve the teacher. Students had to have humility, straightforwardness, intelligence, devotion to divine Reality, discernment and detachment."

*"...the shaping of our own destinies, does not preclude our receiving help from outside; nay, in the vast majority of cases such help is absolutely necessary. When it comes, the higher powers and possibilities of the soul are quickened, spiritual life is awakened, growth is animated, and man becomes holy and perfect in the end. This quickening impulse cannot be derived from books. The soul can only receive impulses from another soul, and from nothing else. We may study books all our lives, we may become very intellectual, but in the end we find that we have not developed at all spiritually.... This inadequacy of books to quicken spiritual growth is the reason why, although almost every one of us can speak most wonderfully on spiritual matters, when it comes to action and the living of a truly spiritual life, we find ourselves so awfully deficient. To quicken the spirit, the impulse must come from another soul."*

### Already Perfected, Past Masters

Another objection often raised to taking a teacher declares that there are illumined beings who attained enlightenment without taking teachers. This is true even in our own era, however, we must ask ourselves, "Is my mind like theirs? Did I exhibit disinterest in the ordinary goals of life from a young age? Did I have a natural ability to meditate and enter samadhi?" We know that great recent teachers like Sri Ramakrishna and Ramana Maharishi either attained illumination before taking teachers or did not have a teacher, respectively. They are examples of rare, highly qualified beings at birth. In the case of Sri Ramakrishna, he later went on to take teachers for different disciplines and religions, as if to show modern people that we must take a spiritual teacher to progress. In both cases, they were already equipped with pure minds, thus qualified minds.

We get an ample view through the Upanisads, Bhagavad Gita, and Itihasa (sacred history of India) of how important a qualified mind is. In fact, the nondual teachings, which today we have at our fingertips via the internet, were only given to those whose minds were ready to receive the knowledge. As the great sage Vasishtha explains, the great Seers throughout time have recognized that *"all souls should be initiated after attaining the four qualifications,"* and that *"Until thy mind is illumined, follow the path of initiation into Brahman shown by illumined souls."* Prospective students of Brahmajnan (knowledge of Brahman, pure Reality) were expected to have control of their senses, tranquility of mind, the ability to forbear heat and cold without complaint. They had to have devotion to truth, nonviolence, gentleness of speech, and be willing to serve the teacher. Students had to have humility, straightforwardness, intelligence, devotion to divine Reality, discernment and detachment. All of these qualities meant that they were sincere of heart and ready for the higher knowledge. And if a student truly longed for spiritual emancipation, mumukshutvam, they would eventually be ushered into the highest teachings of nonduality. The scriptures relate how certain rare beings, endowed with all these qualities from an early age, could hear one of the Mahavakyas (Great Sayings of Nondual Truth), of the Upanisads from a qualified/realized teacher and immediately shed the final veils covering Self-Knowledge. *"Sincere students approach illumined preceptors via prostration, questioning, and selfless service. Then the wise ones, the knowers of Truth, initiate them into the highest wisdom."* (Bhagavad Gita, 4:38)

### Recognition Prior to Realization

Not only do these virtues, above, render one fit for knowledge, they also make it possible to recognize an authentic teacher. Many are the modern seekers who bemoan the teachers of their past, either because they failed to see that person was unqualified, or they failed to recognize that he or she really was qualified and they had missed a great opportunity by chasing lesser ideals or giving up due to impatience, arrogance, or inability to follow instructions. In his Bhakti Sutras, Sage Narada states, *"It is hard to obtain the grace of a great soul, because it is hard to recognize such a one; but if one receives his grace, the effect is infallible."* The qualities of discernment, detachment, tranquility of mind, faith, devotion to truth, humility, etc., ensure that the seeker recognizes that only the Infinite can give ultimate fulfillment. Thus, if one's ultimate goal is Self-Realization or God-Realization, even if one still has earthly desires to fulfill, one will not be led astray by incompetent teachers who mix the world with spirituality.

Sri Ramakrishna has a very poignant story in this regard. He was once walking through the jungle and heard the terrified croaking of a frog. Following the sound, he came across a water snake who had got ahold of a large frog and was trying desperately to swallow it. But the little snake was too small to swallow it down, and thus both were trapped in agony. He used this story to describe the plight of an unqualified teacher trying to help a student get rid of spiritual ignorance. Whereas, if the frog (student) had met with a cobra (highly qualified teacher), it would have made two croaks at most (destruction of the unripe ego that stands in the way of destroying root ignorance). Now, imagine the calamity when both the little snake and the big frog are the same being, as in the case of unqualified practitioners attempting to be their own guide.

The hallmarks of an authentic teacher will also demonstrate to the sincere, reflective aspirant whether or not their own mind is qualified to guide them. Sri Ramakrishna stated that in time

> "....like the rain falling from the one sky onto rooftops fitted with different kinds of rain-spouts, the various human vehicles of this Guru Principle pour forth Truth in torrents or lesser amounts."

one's own mind becomes the guru. We must not be too quick to assume just because "in time" one's own mind can be the guru, that we should trudge on without an embodied teacher, expecting that time itself will somehow ripen the mind! In the *Vivekachudamani*, a scripture by Shankaracharya, he outlines the qualifications of the Guru. The qualities are universal and ought to be considered in all religious traditions according to their particular Ideals. Otherwise, as the saying goes, the blind are leading the blind. It should be noted that in Indian tradition, "Guru" is a principle and not a personality. In the West, we are all too accustomed to personality worship. Sri Ramakrishna explained that Satchidananda, (Existence, Knowledge, Bliss – an epithet for Brahman) is the only Guru. Further, like the rain falling from the one sky onto rooftops fitted with different kinds of rain-spouts, the various human vehicles of this Guru Principle pour forth Truth in torrents or lesser amounts. In another example, a wooden raft can ferry several people across the waters; a sailboat can take more, and an ocean liner can carry thousands of people across the water of the world. These latter, he said, are the great Incarnations and World Teachers.

### The Four Qualifications of the Guru

1 – Akamahata – free from desire. A spiritual teacher should have only one intention for the student, which is that he or she become enlightened. It goes without saying that a true teacher is not seeking personal gratifications in the guru-disciple relationship. On the contrary, the teacher helps the student feel empowered to attain purification of mind through their own self-effort via the methods prescribed. Whereas dependence on the Guru is important, especially in the early and intermediate stages of spiritual life, the student is also expected to use their intelligence and common sense, as Holy Mother has stated.

2 – Shrotriya – knows the essence of the scriptures and can transmit it. This transmission occurs because the teacher has accumulated spiritual power through spiritual practices and realized the truth of what he or she is teaching. Therefore, it exudes off the human vehicle as a subtle power through both words and presence, that uplifts and brings clarity to the minds of those listening with sincerity and faith. Another hallmark of shrotriya is that the guru does not think of it as "my knowledge," because spiritual Truth is eternal. Thus, authentic teachers often appear to have an inexhaustible supply of wisdom.

3 – Avrijina – leads a pure and simple life. The subtle qualities of the teacher get transmitted to the student, therefore, it is important that the teacher be invested with the highest qualities and virtues.

4 – Brahmavid – Is a knower of Brahman. It is in this final qualification that we discover the attainments that mark the difference between one gaining qualification, and one qualified to guide.

Before embarking on that teaching, it should be noted that it may take time for a student to have the ability to perceive the subtle qualities of the fourth qualification. However, if one's teacher or prospective teacher has the first three, one has at least found a respectable dharma teacher.

In the chart provided on the following page, called the *Four Levels of Knowers of Brahman*, we see that the first, and qualifying, level of Brahmavid consists of the first four levels of the Seven Levels of Higher Knowledge. The teaching of the Seven Levels has been passed on for millennia, with various emphases via different teachers. In the scripture, *Yoga Vasishtha*, Sage Vasishtha indicates that the first 3 levels properly endow one with the ability to guide others.

### The Four Levels of Knowers of Brahman

Looking at the first level, some aspirants may find that they have some measure of these early qualities found in **Shubhecha**, Right Aspiration. Shubhecha is naturally based upon discrimination between the Self and what is not the Self (i.e. Prakriti/Nature) and detachment from the non-Self. This detachment serves as an inner GPS that prevents the aspirant from allowing desires and fluctuating states of mind from leading them away from their crucial destination (Self-Realization). Intermediate aspirants may have acquired a solid knowledge of the scriptures, but Wisdom takes assimilation and integration of that knowledge, which is rarely obtainable without recourse to a good teacher.

One who has attained the level of **Vicharana**, Proper Inquiry, understands the nature of Maya. Maya is the covering power of ignorance in the human mind, and also the power that projects what we experience as time, space, and causation, as well as names and forms, all of which veil Atman/Brahman and disguise It as ego, mind, senses, bodies, and elements. Understanding this deeply intensifies one's detachment from phenomena, including the 8 occult powers, and makes way for all virtues to manifest. Quoting Patanjali, Swami Vivekananda wrote to a Western student, *"When a man rejects all the superhuman powers, then he attains to the cloud of virtue."* With this clear and undistracted mind, the aspirant contemplates the Atman, the pure Self within. Although this may have been attempted well before, the Sadhaka (aspirant) has reached a new stage of qualification for this subtlest of meditations.

Attaining the state of **Tanumanasa**, Peaceful Mind, we find a being who has transcended any earthly or heavenly desires, and who can concentrate at will. Not only is concentration present in formal meditation, it has become the default state of mind in all activity. No wonder this is called Peaceful Mind; for a mind that is always concentrated naturally resists intrusions of desire and restlessness. Such beings prefer this state of Peace, as compared to mere happiness and joy dependent upon finite circum-

# THE FOUR LEVELS OF KNOWERS OF BRAHMAN

**The Four Qualities of an Authentic Spiritual Teacher**
*Akamahata* — Devoid of selfish motives
*Shrotriya* — Transmits the essence of the scriptures
*Avrigina* — Leads a pure and simple life
*Brahmavid* — Is a knower of Brahman

## The Four Levels of a Knower of Brahman

| Level 1 | Level 2 | Level 3 | Level 4 |
|---|---|---|---|
| *Brahmavit* | *Brahmavidvara* | *Brahmavidvariya* | *Brahmavidvarishtha* |

### Seven Levels of Higher Knowledge (*Jnana-Bhumikas*)

| | | | |
|---|---|---|---|
| Shubhecha | Shubhecha | Shubhecha | Shubhecha |
| Vicharana | Vicharana | Vicharana | Vicharana |
| Tanumanasa | Tanumanasa | Tanumanasa | Tanumanasa |
| Sattvapati | Sattvapati | Sattvapati | Sattvapati |
| | Asamshakti | Asamshakti | Asamshakti |
| | | Padartha-bhavana | Padartha-bhavana |
| | | | Turiya |

*Shubhecha* — Right Aspiration: possesses detachment, knowledge of scriptures, and wisdom
*Vicharana* — Proper Inquiry: gains all virtues, knows the nature of maya, contemplates Atman
*Tanumanasa* — Peaceful Mind: is free of desire, masters concentration, transcends mind
*Sattvapati* — Virtuous Intelligence: attains renunciation, equality of vision, & nondual Truth
*Asamshakti* — Nonattachment: transcends gunas, becomes jivanmukta, merges in Atman
*Padartha-bhavana* — Grasp of Truth: identifies with Consciousness, sees God in all
*Turiya* — Abidance in the Self: immerses in Brahman, and rest in the disembodied state

"The painful rounds of birth and death in ignorance will never cease until one has reached the first level of jnana-wisdom. To attain that, seek virtue and develop indifference to the world. Then take recourse to the spiritual teachings transmitted by an illumined preceptor." Lord Vasishtha

Copyright 2018, Babaji Bob Kindler

stances. As Holy Mother, Sri Sarada Devi says, *"Peace is the principle thing; one needs peace alone."* Freedom from desires and mastery of concentration leads to transcendence of the mind. The importance of this transcendence cannot be understated. It has been likened to being freed from the confines of a house illumined only by interior lamps, while the sun illumines the house and everything around it.

The fourth level, signifying the state of being a Brahmavid, is called **Sattvapati**. Intelligence is directly illumined by the Atman and the purified mind adheres to Truth. Renunciation is fully mature now, since this realized being perceives the one Reality everywhere, *"the Eternal in all noneternal things."* Such renunciation is truly a deification of all objective and subjective phenomena rather than condemnation or rejection, for the world as something separate from Reality has ceased to exist, and only Reality is perceived in so many forms. This has been described in innumerable exalted ways. In the *Mundako Upanisad*, the rishi exclaims: *"Verily, all this is the immortal Brahman! He is everywhere – above, below, in front, at the back, upon the right, upon the left! All this world is indeed the supreme Brahman."* In our own times, Sri Ramakrishna explained his experience, *"Whatever we see or think about is the manifestation of the glory of the Primordial Energy, the primeval Consciousness. Creation, preservation, and destruction, living beings and the universe, and further, meditation and the meditator, bhakti and prema – all these are manifestations of the glory of that Power."* (Gospel of Sri Ramakrishna, p. 290)

## Conclusion

An exploration of these first three to four levels of Higher Knowledge reveal what a lofty station the role of guru and spiritual guide is. Finding such a teacher is a rare good fortune; being able to recognize such a guide requires that the student be endowed with essential qualifications. As the *Katha Upanisad* says, *"Even to hear of It (the Atman) is not available to many; many, even having heard of It, cannot comprehend. Wonderful is its teacher, and equally clever the pupil. Wonderful indeed is the one who comprehends it when taught by an able preceptor."* (v.2:7)

Annapurna Sarada is the president of SRV Associations and an assistant teacher for the sangha. She also writes on spiritual topics at Medium.com.

**Svayambhuva's Transmission of The Seven Levels of Knowledge**

Shubhecha – Right Aspiration

Vicharana – Proper Inquiry

Tanumanasa – Peaceful Mind

Sattvapati – Illumined Intelligence

Asamsakti – Nonattachment

Padartha-bhavana – Grasp of Truth

Turiya – Abidance in the Self

Turiyatita – Pure Consciousness

# Live-Streaming Class Series from SRV Hawaii for 2021

### ▪ Shankara's Spiritual Brilliance
#### May, 2nd, & 9th, 2021

*Born in the light of the Atman, coming to full remembrance of his divinity at 6 years of age, recalling all the scriptures and their wisdom at 8 years old, Shankara was the full incarnation of Siva whose guru, Govindapada, was a reincarnation of Patanjali, the Father of Yoga, some 500 years earlier. Govindapada's guru was none other than Gaudapada, the fully illumined Advaita Vedantist, whose incarnation helped India rise out of a fallen Buddhist era to reclaim her original tradition of the Vedas and Upanisads that, itself, had been in a poor state of affairs at the time of Lord Buddha's birth in India around 550 B.C. In this two-part class series Shankara's life will be taken up, centering around the main events that transpired through his 32 years of life in the physical frame. Additionally, some of his key teachings will be presented, giving all a fuller vision of who he was and his great import to the world of religion and philosophy.*

### ▪ Streaming Particles of Living Intelligence
#### June 13th, & 20th, 2021

*Termed "Jnana Matras" in the ancient Sanskrit language, these powerful particles of conscious Awareness act in the inner realms much the same way that the sun acts on the physical plane, bestowing life and warmth upon the planet. Originating as wisdom rays off of The Word, AUM/OM, these increments of living intelligence bathe the minds of The Trinity, the seers and rishis, the gods and goddesses, and thereby work their way out to the heavens of the celestials, ancestors, and humanity itself. All that is clear, knowledgeable, beneficial, and ingenious manifests and expresses itself due to the force of these minute unseen units. They are smaller than atoms, and much more powerful, for they are not found in matter, but in mind. Living beings who become qualified to perceive and utilize jnana matras are those whose understanding of deep intellectual and philosophical principles is natural and spontaneous. Beyond even that, the soul seeking freedom from Nature and other limitations can flow with streams of these particles to the Source of Awareness, merging into Formless Reality. In this two-class series, a jnana matra will be taken apart, as far as possible, and its inherent qualities inspected to reveal the secret of pure, conscious Awareness.*

### ▪ Think Small:
#### Prana, Tanmatras, & Psychic Prana
#### July 11th, 18th, & 25th, 2021

*On the heels of the three-part class series on Jnana Matras, and following up on their role in spinning out the worlds of name and form in time and space, the subjects of prana and tanmatras will receive attention and inspection. Swami Vivekananda has said to us, when he was present, recently, in the body for 39 years, that the world, particularly the West, was not "in the know" about subtle matter and its role in life, and in the life of the Spirit as well. Two tattvas, cosmic principles, received special mention from him in this regard: those of prana and tanmatras. Without knowledge of these — life-force and subtle matter — an internal life as mentioned by Jesus and other great luminaries would simply not be possible. This gives rise and credence to the declaration that mankind today simply does not possess a spiritual life, for the subtle channels that lead inwards and beyond matter are verily stopped up, and cannot conduct the flow of prana and subtle intelligent particles which lead to, say, "The Kingdom of Heaven Within." Lord Kapila, the Father of the Sankhya Darhana, called this problem "Samsara-Prag-Bhara" in his age and time, like a broad river of souls that has been dammed up. The Brahma Granthi, Vishnu Granthi, Rudra Granthi, and the infamous "Curtain of Nescience" — all coverings over*

## Live-Streaming Class Series, continued

*the mind — are thickened and made practically impassable to spiritually seeking souls due to ignorance of tattvas such as prana and tanmatras. Fortunately, illumined souls with great power, like Vivekananda, can force an opening in major nadis using his mastery of prana and psychic prana. Three classes on this important but rather unknown subject will afford an opportunity for aspiring souls to see and recover their knowledge and mastery of prana and psychic prana, a subject which, at present, is little more than an association with mere breathing exercises in the minds of contemporary humanity.*

### ▪ Bussho Ox-Herding & Atmic Lion Taming:
### Zen's Jugyu-No-Zu & Vedanta's Atma Vichara
#### August 8th, 15th, & 22nd, 2021

*Bussho in Zen, Atman in Vedanta; who can tell the difference? Possibly the methods of each tradition utilized to reach realization of Them are the same. Or are they? They are both described by seers who have experienced Them as being beyond matter, unfixed, nondual, devoid of mass, beyond birth and death, beyond individuality, personality, imagination, and conceptualization, etc. Both traditions insist, as well, that the aspirant is to learn to live in Them, thereby reaching the Final Goal of Liberation — Nirvana/Nirvikalpa. This class series will look at the well-known stages of Ox-Herding in conjunction with how Vedanta utilizes practices such as Sadhanachatushtaya and Atma Vichara to achieve its consummate End.*

### ▪ The Gunas of Prakriti & The Vrittis of Yoga
#### September 5th, 12th, & 19th, 2021

*The discovery of the gunas of Prakriti by the Indian rishis goes back to the period of Sankhya, if not earlier. How everything, animate and inanimate by today's measure and standard, is influenced by balance, movement, and inertia, is a key bit of knowledge to possess. But India's seers were not so interested in how nature writhed under these modes, and instead began to view them as properties of the mind that influenced the moods of living beings, both for better and for worse. Vrittis, those waves of the mind that rise and fall continually, were also a key player in India's development of its superb yoga psychology, and how the gunas influenced the mind's thoughts became both an art for observing them and a practice in overcoming them — mastered in the end by perfect control of thoughts followed by their dissolution in meditation. Gunas and vrittis together will make up the substance of this class series, revealing valuable teachings for serious students of Yoga and Vedanta.*

### ▪ Kaivalya Upanisad & The Shatarudriya
#### October 17th, 24th, 31st, & November 7th, 2021

*Among some of the more well-known "minor" Upanisads, the Kaivalya Upanisad finds its important place, transmitting, as it does, the deepest wisdom concerning the highest state of Awareness. In a four-class series, providing time to cover its brief but potent slokas, the scripture's main section will be scrutinized, also taking up its minute but crucial second section concerning the worship of Lord Siva in reference to the Shatarudriya, which are a collection of famous verses found in the Yajur Veda and chanted by millions of souls for devotion to the Lord and purification of mind.*

### ▪ Bhartrihari's 100 Verses on Renunciation
#### November 28th, & December 5th, 2021

*Being one of Swami Vivekananda's favorite spiritual poems, Bhartrihari's collection of verses capture the spirit of mature renunciation without sacrificing any of the soul's heartfelt devotion or the high art of true poetry. This three part class series will take up certain of the more potent expressions found in the work, including the lofty and practical wisdom that is woven into many of the verses. The deep earthly lessons that Bhartrihari learned in life, and which he put into two other 100 verse poems he composed that contained less of spiritual content, gets reflected in the repeated final line of every verse of this poem, mainly, that "....only renunciation is fearless...."*

\* Livestream.com/BabajiBobKindler

# SRV Vedanta Associations — Babaji's Teaching Schedule, 2021

**SRV Hawai'i**
Administrative Office
PO Box 1364
Honoka'a, HI 96727

**SRV Associations'**
Website: www.srv.org
Online Ashram:
srvwisdom.org
Email: srvinfo@srv.org
Phone: 808-990-3354

**SRV Oregon**
1922 SE 42nd Ave.,
Portland, Oregon
808-990-3354

For Livestream & Zoom events go to www.srv.org and sign our email list

## May, 2021

**SRV Oregon**

- 5/22 Sat 9:30am Class: Amrita-Nada Upanisad
- 6:00pm Arati/Satsang with Babaji
- 5/23 Sun 9:30am Class: Amrita-Nada Upanisad
- 5/26 Wed 7:00pm Bhagavad Gita with Anurag
- 5/28 - 6/1 SRV Retreat at Windwood Waters

Weekend Classes also on Livestream, 9:30 am to 12:30 pm, PDT

---

**SRV Memorial Day Retreat, May 28 — June 1st**
**Subject:** Patanjali's 8-Limbed Yoga
Select Sutras with In-depth Teachings
Location: Windwood Waters
Arrive Friday night 28th, depart Tuesday Noon, 6/1
For retreat details, see Page 55

---

**June 26th & 27th: Online Seminar — Extracting Essence**

## July, 2021

**SRV Hawai'i**

**SRV Independence Day Retreat, July 1st — 5th**
**Subject:** Vivekananda's Vedanta
& Ramakrishna's New Dispensation
A Thorough Grounding in the Teachings of
The Great Swan & The Great Swami
Arrive Thursday night, July 1st, depart Monday, 5th, at Noon
For details on all retreats, see Retreat Page 57

---

**Aug 28th & 29th: Online Seminar — How Vedanta Works**

## October, 2021

**SRV Oregon**

- 10/2 Sat 9:30 Class: Amrita-Nada Upanisad
- 6:00 Arati/Satsang with Babaji
- 10/3 Sun 9:30am Class: Amrita-Nada Upanisad
- 10/6 Wed 7:00pm Bhagavad Gita with Anurag

---

**SRV Columbus Day Retreat, October 7th — 11th**
**Subject:** Annapurna Upanisad
SRV's Study of the 7th "Divine Mother" Upanisad
Location: TBA
Arrive Thursday night, 7th, depart Monday Noon, 11th
For retreat details, see page 56

---

**Nov 20th & 21st: Online Seminar — Nonviolence on Earth**

## December, 2021

**SRV Hawai'i**

**SRV December Retreat, December 16th — 20th**
**Subject:** Tantra & Vedanta
The Two Great Streams & Their Assets
Arrive Thursday night Dec 16th, depart 20th at Noon
For retreat details, see page 57

---

**Hawai'i's Sunday Live Streaming Classes,
2:30 - 5:30pm HST**
Hawai'i SRV Ashram   Directions: Call: 808-990-3354

▪**The Soul Bound is Man,
that Same Soul Free is God**
April 4th, 11th, & 18th, 2021

▪**Shankara's Spiritual Brilliance**
May 2nd & 9th, 2021

▪**Streaming Particles of Living Intelligence**
June 13th, & 20th, 2021

▪**Think Small**
Prana, Tanmatras, & Psychic Prana
July 11th, 18th, & 25th, 2021

▪**Bussho Ox-Herding & Atmic Lion Taming**
Zen's Jugyo-No-Zu & Vedanta's Atma Vichara
August 8th, 15th, 22nd, 2021

▪**The Gunas of Prakriti & The Vrittis of Yoga**
September 5th, 12th, & 19th, 2021

▪**Kaivalya Upanisad & The Shatarudriya**
October 17th, 24th, 31st, & Nov 7th, 2021

▪**Bhartrihari's 100 Verses on Renunciation**
November 28th, & Dec 5th, 2021

---

**Weekly Saturday Events with Babaji
Held Via Zoom**

Satsang — join us for Q&A
Saturdays at 8am HST

Brahman Bytes —
Group Philosophical Discussion
Saturdays at 10am HST on srvwisdom.org

To participate: Sign our email list at SRV.org

---

**Announcing SRV India Pilgrimage**
**Date TBA    Inquire for Reservation & Further Information**

**Destinations: Himalayas, Varanasi, Delhi, Kolkata, & Chennai**  (contact Babaji - babaji@hialoha.net)

# SRV Vedanta Associations Online Seminar Schedule 2021

# SRV Websites:
# www.srv.org
# community.SRVWisdom.org

### SRV Online Seminars

**June 26th & 27th**
**Extracting Essence from Daily Actions**

In this online seminar, the subtle art of transforming every day activities into direct spiritual experience will be taken up, along with wise ways to avoid mere habitual living for the sake of pleasurable existence alone.

**August 28th & 29th: (Janmashtami)**
**How Advanced Vedantic Tools Work**

With the growing interest in Vedanta, students are wanting to know more about how its practices — like adhyaropa and apavada — get applied, and how vivarta gets removed in order to afford clear vision.

**November 20th & 21th:**
**Establishing Ahimsa/Nonviolence on Earth**

In a war-torn world, where even periods of peace are rare in today's times, the need for maintaining nonviolence as both a sound policy and a given human right will be explored. The peaceful and productive lives of illumined beings will be exemplified, revealing how ahimsa is actually a divine quality rather than just a political alternative.

### *SRV Social Media Pages*

facebook.com/srvvedanta
youtube.com/c/SrvOrg
instagram.com/srvassociations

### Explore www.SRV.org and discover:
- Sanskrit Chants to learn/practice
- Devotional Songs
- "In the Spirit" Audio Interviews

Teachings:
- SRV's Teachings for Youth/Children

Nectar Magazine:
Order back issues of Nectar

Links to Video & Live Classes:
- SRV's Livestream Channel
- Webcast Timezone Schedule
- YouTube Channel

**Be Sure to Sign our Email List!**

### Join SRVWisdom.org & find all these in one place:
- All of Babaji's video classes
- Online Archive of audio Discourses
- Online Archive of Nectar's back issues
- Easy access to all live online events
- Babaji's Godblogs: Brahman Bytes
- Many special Features
- Spiritual Community!
- Membership comes with special discounts for books, charts, and in-person retreats.

### SRV YouTube Channel Class Series
- Advaita of the Avatars
- Destroying the Rust of Spiritual Life
- Advaita Vedanta's Six Proofs of Truth
- The Wisdom Particle
- Tibetan Buddhism & Advaita Vedanta
- Spiritual Interviews
- Engaging Music Videos
- Satsangs with Babaji
- ...and so much more

# SRV Associations — Retreats for 2021

## SRV Windwood Waters Retreat on Yoga
### May 28th - June 1st, 2021, Stevenson, WA
### Retreat Topic: *Patanjali's 8-Limbed Yoga*

The noble Eight-Limbed Yoga of Lord Patanjali (also called Raja Yoga, Ashtanga Yoga, and Patanjala) has still to fully arrive in the West, and this is due, in part, to Europe and America's preoccupation with yoga of a physical kind only. In this retreat the emphasis will begin with teachings on the basic features on yama and niyama, such as nonviolence, study of scriptures, and deep devotion to God. The five crucial steps in between the first two limbs and the eighth — Raja Yoga's crowning glory of Samadhi — will also receive a detailed scrutiny so as to ensure a full understanding of this most comprehensive spiritual pathway.

This retreat on Yoga occurs just prior to the release of SRV's new book, *Atmic Testament on Yoga*, which is planned for publishing in 2001-2002.

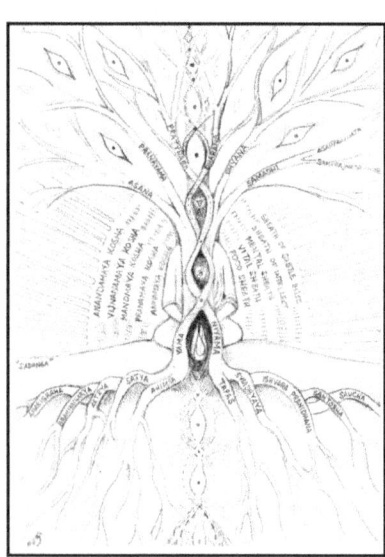

**Space Limited:**

* Location: Windwood Waters retreat site near Stevenson, WA
* Arrival: Friday, May 28th, by 9:00 pm
* Departure: Tuesday, June 1, noon

* Tuition (all-inclusive): Full Rate $690; full time Students $425; Financial hardship? Call 808-990-3354

Members of the online ashram (paying full rate) who then paid the full tuition for the last Hawaii retreat are eligible for ½ off the tuition portion of this retreat, a savings of: $225. (And if this is your first in-person retreat since becoming a member, your next one will get this discount)

# SRV Fall Columbus Day Retreat, 2021
## Over the Auspicious Time of Navaratri, Durga Puja

October 7th – 11th, 2021
Location: TBA
Subject: *The Seven Goddess Upanisads: Annapurna Upanisad, Pt.1*

The SRV Sangha and Friends have studied the Devi Upanisad, Sita Upanisad, Saubaghya Lakshmi Upanisad, Savitri Upanisad, Yoga Kundalini Upanisad, and the Tripura Upanisad over 6 Autumn retreats. The 7th feather in our scriptural cap of Mother Upanisads will be Part 1 of a deep inspection of the Annapurna Upanisad. Prior attendance not required

**Location:** TBA
**Arrival:** Thursday, Oct 7th, 6pm
**Departure:** Monday, Oct 11th, 12:00 noon
**Tuition:** Adults: $450 / Full Time Students: $225 / Lodging/Meals, TBA
**Registration:** Begins now. Tuition by September 7th
**Financial hardship?** Call 808-990-3354 to discuss options
**Register by email:** srvinfo@srv.org  or by phone 808-990-3354

# Dharma Weekends with SRV Associations
Livestream, Zoom, & in-person with
## Babaji Bob Kindler, Spiritual Director

**Saturdays at 8:00am HST**
On Zoom

## Satsang
Join us for Q & A
Bring your questions from classes and studies

**Saturdays at 10:00am HST**
On Zoom via SRV's online Ashram
community.srvwisdom.org

## Brahman Bytes
In the Aftermath of the Avataric Descent
Group Philosophical Discussion

**Sundays at 2:30pm HST**
On Livestream & in person

## New Class Series each Month
(Most Sundays, see schedule p.53)

Schedule Subject to Change

## Join SRV's email list to receive schedule notices, visit SRV.org

# SRV Associations — Hawaii Retreat #1 for 2021

July 1st - July 5th, 2021, On Vivekananda's Mahasamadhi (4th), Prior to Gurupurnima
Retreat Topic: *Vivekananda's Vedanta & Ramakrishna's "New Dispensation"*

As a recently composed inspirational hymn of India sings, "A New Man has come." And the news of His coming is that He has brought to the people of this age of awakening a "new dispensation," which translates as a fresh seeding of the eternal truths of India's timeless dharmic scriptures. An inspirational light has now been cast upon all of the world's religious traditions, highlighting the perfect nature of aspiring humanity, as contrasted to its previously misinterpreted "sinful" nature.

Along with the 16 illumined souls who attended upon this unique spiritual event, and a host of other devotees of God, one in particular walked over the world and spread the message of inherent Oneness directly to benighted humanity. Swami Vivekananda's testament to Nondual Truth and Philosophy will form the main element of this high-minded retreat in the Hawaiian Islands, on the "Big Island," surrounded by the vast body of healing waters we call Ganga Pacifica — a fitting location to immerse body, mind, and soul in breathtaking clarification.

*"Without studying Ramakrishna Paramahamsa, one can never understand the real import of the Vedas, the Vedanta, of the Bhagavata, and the other Puranas. His life is a searchlight of infinite power thrown upon the whole mass of Indian religious thought. He was the living commentary of the Vedas and to their aim. He lived in one life the whole cycle of the national religious existence in India. The older Teachers were no doubt good, but this is the new religion of this age — the synthesis of Yoga, Knowledge, Devotion and Work — the propagation of Knowledge and Devotion down to the very lowest, without distinction of age or sex. The previous Incarnations were all right, but they have been synthesized in the person of Ramakrishna."*

**Location:** SRV Retreat Center on the Hamakua Coast, Big Island of Hawaii
**Arrival:** Thurs, July 1st, by 6pm
**Departure:** Monday, July 5th, at 12:00 noon
**Tuition, Meals, & Lodging:** Shared rooms, $515/person; Private room, $565; Tenting, $415-465/person
**Registration:** Begins now. Tuition is due by June 9th
**Register by email:** srvinfo@srv.org or by phone 808-990-3354
**Financial hardship?** Contact us to learn about options.

Student Rates (full time students:
Shared Room — $360
Tenting — $260-210 (Same rates for Retreat #2)

# SRV Associations — Hawaii Retreat #2 for 2021

December 16th - 20th, 2021, Big Island of Hawaii
Retreat Topic: *Tantra & Vedanta — The Two Great Streams*

Worship and Wisdom, Devotion and Discrimination, have always characterized the two main elements of religion and philosophy in India, with meditation and action supporting and complementing them. Flowing like mighty rivers — side by side at times and merging their waters at others — these powerful pathways of divine deification and deep discernment have refined and fulfilled seeking souls for cycles of time unending. Heart-based Love of God and mind-expanding Knowledge of Nonduality then transforms life into an expression of matured spirituality that maintains human awareness at a very lofty vibrational level.

How does Vedanta work its transformative effects on the human mind; what special tools does it apply in order to purify the mental level and transport consciousness into those sublime areas of living intelligence? And what is the secret of Tantra's ability to change the poison of relativity into the Nectar of Nonduality, doing so via sublimation and deification rather than the route of outright renunciation taken by the acetics? This intriguing twofold subject will get scrutinized for the benefit of all in attendance, shedding light on these two Eternal Paths.

**Location:** Hamakua, Big Island of Hawaii
**Arrival:** Thursday, December 16th, by 6pm  /  **Departure:** Monday, December 20th, at 12:00 noon
**Tuition, Meals, & Lodging:** Shared rooms, $515/person; Private room, $565; Tenting, $415-465/person
**Registration:** Begins now. Tuition is due by November 27th
**Register by email:** srvinfo@srv.org or by phone 808-990-3354  **Financial hardship?** Contact us to learn options.

*Advaita-satya-amritam*

# NECTAR
## Of Non-Dual Truth

**Donation/Order Form**
*Suggested donation $15 per issue*

*Order Nectar #37 by January 15, 2022 for free delivery in the U.S. Order online at www.srv.org > magazine*
*Or, use this subscription card, email, or call us!*
*Your donation will help make Nectar available to others.*

☐ Please send me/my friend/spiritual center a free copy of the next issue of Nectar.
☐ Send me ____ copies to give to friends, Spiritual Centers, or a business of my choice. (fill out back of form)
☐ I want to make sure there are future issues of Nectar ($200 and up)

*Nectar needs sustaining donors! Your gift is tax-deductible.*

Please fill out the back side of this form and mail it with your check to:
SRV Associations, PO Box 1364, Honokaa, HI 96727 *(payable to: SRV Associations)*
MasterCard or Visa accepted online at www.srv.org > Giving
808-990-3354 • srvinfo@srv.org • www.srv.org

#36

---

*Advaita-satya-amritam*

# NECTAR
## Of Non-Dual Truth

**Donation/Order Form**
*Suggested donation $15 per issue*

*Order Nectar #37 by January 15, 2022 for free delivery in the U.S. Order online at www.srv.org > magazine*
*Or, use this subscription card, email, or call us!*
*Your donation will help make Nectar available to others.*

☐ Please send me/my friend/spiritual center a free copy of the next issue of Nectar.
☐ Send me ____ copies to give to friends, Spiritual Centers, or a business of my choice. (fill out back of form)
☐ I want to make sure there are future issues of Nectar ($200 and up)

*Nectar needs sustaining donors! Your gift is tax-deductible.*

Please fill out the back side of this form and mail it with your check to:
SRV Associations, PO Box 1364, Honokaa, HI 96727 *(payable to: SRV Associations)*
MasterCard or Visa accepted online at www.srv.org > Giving
808-990-3354 • srvinfo@srv.org • www.srv.org

#36

---

*Advaita-satya-amritam*

# NECTAR
## Of Non-Dual Truth

**Donation/Order Form**
*Suggested donation $15 per issue*

*Order Nectar #37 by January 15, 2022 for free delivery in the U.S. Order online at www.srv.org > magazine*
*Or, use this subscription card, email, or call us!*
*Your donation will help make Nectar available to others.*

☐ Please send me/my friend/spiritual center a free copy of the next issue of Nectar.
☐ Send me ____ copies to give to friends, Spiritual Centers, or a business of my choice. (fill out back of form)
☐ I want to make sure there are future issues of Nectar ($200 and up)

*Nectar needs sustaining donors! Your gift is tax-deductible.*

Please fill out the back side of this form and mail it with your check to:
SRV Associations, PO Box 1364, Honokaa, HI 96727 *(payable to: SRV Associations)*
MasterCard or Visa accepted online at www.srv.org > Giving
808-990-3354 • srvinfo@srv.org • www.srv.org

#36

*Your Shipping information:* (if ordering by mail)

Name: _____

Address: _____

City, State, Zip: _____

Email: _____

*Additional Address:* (please use a sheet of paper for more addresses)

Name: _____

Address: _____

City, State, Zip: _____

Email: _____

**MasterCard or Visa accepted online at www.srv.org > Giving**

Or you can pay by credit card over the phone.

808-990-3354 • srvinfo@srv.org • www.srv.org

Questions? Call or write us!

---

*Your Shipping information:* (if ordering by mail)

Name: _____

Address: _____

City, State, Zip: _____

Email: _____

*Additional Address:* (please use a sheet of paper for more addresses)

Name: _____

Address: _____

City, State, Zip: _____

Email: _____

**MasterCard or Visa accepted online at www.srv.org > Giving**

Or you can pay by credit card over the phone.

808-990-3354 • srvinfo@srv.org • www.srv.org

Questions? Call or write us!

---

*Your Shipping information:* (if ordering by mail)

Name: _____

Address: _____

City, State, Zip: _____

Email: _____

*Additional Address:* (please use a sheet of paper for more addresses)

Name: _____

Address: _____

City, State, Zip: _____

Email: _____

**MasterCard or Visa accepted online at www.srv.org > Giving**

Or you can pay by credit card over the phone.

808-990-3354 • srvinfo@srv.org • www.srv.org

Questions? Call or write us!

www.ingramcontent.com/pod-product-compliance
Lightning Source LLC
Chambersburg PA
CBHW081402080526
44588CB00016B/2571